THE PAPACY AND FASCISM

AMS PRESS
NEW YORK

THE
PAPACY AND FASCISM
THE CRISIS OF THE TWENTIETH CENTURY

By
F. A. Ridley

" Let him be anathema who affirms that the Roman Pontiff can and ought to reconcile and adapt himself to progress, to Liberalism, and to modern culture."—H. H. POPE PIUS IX, Syllabus of Condemned Errors attached to Encyclical " Quanta Cura ", 1864.

" For Heaven be thanked ! each new attraction
Is still attended by—Reaction ! "
IBSEN, *Brand*, Act V.

LONDON
MARTIN SECKER WARBURG LTD
22 ESSEX STREET STRAND
1937

Library of Congress Cataloging in Publication Data

Ridley, Francis A   1897–
    The papacy and fascism.

    Reprint of the 1937 ed.
    1. Papacy––History. 2. Socialism and Catholic
Church. 3. Fascism and Catholic Church. 4. Catholic
Church––Relations (diplomatic) I. Title.
BX1790.R5 1973   262'.13   72–180422
ISBN 0-404-56156-X

Reprinted from the edition of 1937, London
First AMS edition published in 1973
Manufactured in the United States of America

AMS PRESS INC.
NEW YORK, N. Y.   10003

PREFACE

It has been the function of modern civilization not merely to sponsor the idea of evolution but also to put it into practice in every sphere of intellectual and social life; a process which reaches its culmination in the social and intellectual movement of the twentieth century. The same unequalled facility for progress has, however, generated a reaction of corresponding dimensions. This reaction assumes to-day two main forms, one old and the other new, the Roman Catholic Church, and Fascism, the great reactionary force of the present time. These two "Black Internationals" play the part of the two leading obstacles to social and scientific progress in the contemporary civilized world. Differing in the circumstances of their origin and in character, they are united by common enemies, common hatreds, and in particular by a common atavism that seeks to put back to a bygone hour the clock of human progress.

The following pages are a study of the Catholic-Fascist alliance, the "Holy Alliance", as it is here called, of spiritual, cultural, and political reaction. To achieve the end of this study, the analysis is divided into three parts dealing in turn with complementary aspects of the question. We begin with the Papacy, an historic force which, while temporarily eclipsed by the current notoriety of Fascist politics, is by far the more homogeneous, stable, and consequently dangerous in the permanent sense, of the two allies. The Papacy has outlived many "Fascisms" in the past; it has survived many institutions and régimes far more firmly based and composed of materials far more durable than the flashy demagogy and opportunist makeshifts of Mussolini and the Third Reich. As it is, the Rome of the Vatican will probably survive the tawdry magnificence of the Rome of neo-Cæsarism and of its still more shoddy imitators.

The Papacy is, of all contemporary institutions, the most deeply rooted in history; its tendrils stretch down deep into the past, and the institution could not, indeed, be conceived as the creation of modern ideas; its world philosophy is anterior to, and distinct from, all modern conceptions.[1] If, therefore, we would study the reactions of Rome to the contemporary crisis, the crisis of the twentieth century, we must see what was the nature of her reactions in the past to the similarly deep crises which have marked her long and stormy passage through the ages.

The first part of the present investigation is devoted, accordingly, to an enquiry into the crises through which Rome has passed in former days, and into the technique which she progressively evolved to meet and to overcome them. Only so can justice be done to the events at present taking place; only so can a wide and accurate perspective

[1] " The Papacy, based as it is on mediæval ideas, has maintained and in many ways increased its moral power and influence, in an atmosphere which is repugnant to it, in the midst of social and political institutions, tendencies and ideas to which it is fundamentally opposed." J. B. BURY, *History of the Papacy in the Nineteenth Century.*

be secured in the light of which present events, and Rome's reaction to them, can be viewed in proper proportions. It is, after all, no accident that *semper eadem*—" for ever the same "—remains still, as in the past, the vaunted motto of the Roman Church and the See of Peter.

In the second and third parts are presented, in due sequence, the essential features of the crisis, pre-eminently of Socialism and of " Social Evolution ", and the " Holy Alliance " of Catholicism and Fascism which constitutes the Papal solution of that crisis. Of these it need only be remarked that the author applies to Socialism and Fascism alike the same historical method used in the first part with respect to the Papacy.

Neither of these warring creeds is treated as primarily political, still less in an ephemeral party sense. Contrarily, Socialism is presented as the logical culminating step of modern evolution and of modern civilization. Fascism, likewise, is offered to the reader as the extreme and logical form of the modern reaction, which can achieve the destruction of Socialism only by destroying the whole of modern civilization, of which that phenomenon represents the final and logically sequent term. Thus the Papacy, ecclesiastical " Fascism ", and Fascism, political " Catholicism ", have a common aim and common enemies ; features which ensure their common historical rôle and action in the circumstances of the twentieth century, to whatever extent those points of disharmony noted and commented on in the text may subsequently appear to dissolve their alliance.

It may be observed in conclusion that the

author makes no pretence to an impartiality as impossible as it would be ludicrous. In the conflict between the apes and the angels, signalized by Disraeli, he holds that it is better to be a risen ape than a fallen angel. But anti-Catholic and anti-Fascist as the ensuing pages are, the author has studied seriously even hostile phenomena, and in particular has sought to judge the points at issue by responsible documents, and not by the " wild and whirling words " of commentators or of irresponsible partisans. Hence, he has relied chiefly on Papal encyclicals and the well-considered views of weighty historians, and, in the case of Fascism, of outstanding Fascist leaders.

The great reactionary alliance of our times is a sinister, but serious and important subject. If only on the principle that one must understand one's enemy in order effectually to combat him, the matter is one deserving of serious study, not only by the professed devotees of modern progress, but by all thoughtful people who enjoy the achievements and possibilities inherent in that rationalist and evolutionary civilization which arose in spite of Catholicism, and will endure in spite of Fascism —the support of the Infallible Pope notwithstanding.

In order to ensure correctness, exact references are given to authorities where possible ; notes are generally placed at the end of the chapter or section to which they refer.

CONTENTS

INTRODUCTION

An over-optimistic theory, once current in educated circles, regarded the decline and eventual disappearance of religion as a foregone conclusion which would inevitably come about from the natural progress of mankind, consequent upon the advent of an age of science and of political freedom. The events, of the post-war era, and in particular of the last few years, so disheartening to believers in human progress, have rendered this concept no longer tenable. The forces of reaction have displayed an unexpected toughness and vitality, and, as so often before in history, the children of this world have proved, if not wiser, at least stronger than the children of light. The state of the world to-day, a state whose unhappiness has now passed into the domain of the platitudinous, affords an unanswerable proof that this is indeed so, and that the march of progress is more gradual and follows a more circuitous route than was supposed by the over-optimistic generation of Darwin, Macaulay and Buckle.

As in the Manichean Dualism of the ancient East, the beneficent Ormuzd, God of light, whose mission it is to enlighten the path of humanity, finds his efforts hampered and his path obstructed by the dark forces of the nether world, of the maleficent empire of Ahriman, the co-equal spirit of evil, so Reaction, and reaction not merely political, but extending to every sphere of human culture and behaviour, now threatens humanity all too plainly with reversion to the primitive and with the triumph of atavism in every sphere.

Even in the optimistic mid-nineteenth century, Macaulay had already noticed and remarked upon the extraordinary powers of recovery which have been manifested throughout the course of its long and chequered history by the Roman Catholic Church, that arch-reactionary in the religious field, and by the Papacy, for so long the avowed adversary of every type and effort of human progress in morals and in culture, no less than in politics and in religion. So much did this faculty of re-silience in the Roman See strike the great Whig historian that, as is well known, he virtually donned the mantle of a clairvoyant, and, forgetful both of the facts of human transiency and of the dictates of historical prudence, predicted a quasi-eternal duration for the Roman See and Church—that Church which had already survived all the institu-tions of the world that had witnessed the rise of Western European civilization and would, so Macaulay professed to think, survive its collapse, and the transference of the centres of human culture to the antipodes.[1]

[1] " She saw the commencement of all the governments and of all the ecclesiastical institutions that now exist in the world ; and we feel no assurance that she is not destined to see the end of them all. She was great and respected before the Saxon had set foot in Britain, before the Frank had crossed the Rhine, when Grecian eloquence still flourished in Antioch, when idols were still worshipped in the temple of Mecca. And she may still exist in undiminished vigour when some traveller from New Zealand shall, in the midst of a vast solitude, take his stand on a broken arch of London Bridge to sketch the ruins of St. Paul's."—MACAULAY, *Essay on Ranke's " History of the Popes "*.

In making this daring and dramatic prediction, the great Victorian no doubt allowed his usual bias towards excessive optimism to swing with his customary violence of expression too far in a pessimistic direction. As a more sober German critic of Macaulay has shrewdly remarked, there is no warrant for mistaking even the strongest of historic institutions—as the Papacy may reasonably be held to have been—for something eternal and beyond human comparison or mortality. None the less, the Papacy has, without doubt, manifested a most remarkable vitality throughout all the phases of its career, and has hitherto demonstrated an ability without equal for recovering from seemingly hopeless positions and for unexpectedly re-emerging from the shadow of defeat and decay in a triumphant and spectacular return to the centre of human affairs.[1]

Nor at any time or place has the church of the apostolic fisherman lost the piscatory art practised by its founder, particularly that department of it which consists in fishing in troubled waters. And the waters of Europe and of human civilization were never more troubled than they are to-day.

Hitherto, the history of the Roman Papacy, the most reactionary and the strongest of all religious institutions, has centred around a series of crises which, differing in their incidence, but alike in their severity, have in turn threatened the bark of Peter with destruction. Armed with a marvellous power of adaptability and with knowledge of the constant elements in human nature—the fruit of vast and varied experience of mankind

[1] Krüger, *The Papacy.*

and its affairs—the Papacy has devised methods suitable to meet and to overcome each successive crisis, and has emerged from the shadow of death as strong as, or stronger than, she was before.

Nor is there any reason to believe that the Papal See has lost either its desire for life or the cunning requisite to ensure it. Indeed, if the most essential science is the science of survival, the Roman Church has never failed to be super-scientific. The Roman Catholic Church, with a longer history than any other Western institution behind it, is the most faithful to history of all those institutions ; there is no organization, in the Western world at least, which has remained more faithful to its essential type than has the Papal organization. It is, indeed, its unvarying fidelity to type that has permitted it to be always so adaptable in detail.

Consequently the future of the Papacy can be judged from its past. It would be, therefore, as rash to infer that the Roman Catholic Church will founder in the heavy seas that accompany the crisis of the twentieth century, as it would have been to infer in the sixteenth century that the terrific storms which then beat upon the Vatican were destined to bury the Papacy for ever in its ruins. The antithesis of Darwinism in its dogmatic creed and in its world outlook, the Roman Catholic Church is in a certain sense the supreme example of Darwinian evolution, in that its will to survive is equalled only by its supreme efficiency in finding, and in following to a successful issue, in the labyrinth of difficulties which surround it, the path that does actually lead to a happy way of escape.

This faculty for seeking and finding a way of escape from the environment of menacing crisis the Papacy now, when confronted by the crisis of the twentieth century, as formerly in the successive crises that marked her earlier centuries, retains and hopes to use, for it would be to reason without any regard either for abstract logic or for concrete history to suppose that the Roman Church and its Papal rulers have become so enfeebled with age as not to desire survival, or so mentally inert as to have neglected to consult either the lessons of their own long past or the vast stores of human wisdom stored up in the treasure house of Peter—the profound memory of nineteen centuries of human cunning and experience, now as formerly available for her salvation.

If any one thing can be predicted with absolute assurance, it is that the Roman Church will not give up the ghost without a struggle. If she has eventually to go down to destruction, if, in a word, she is, in spite of her grandiose claims, human after all, and not divine, at least she will not permit herself to draw this conclusion, and to submit to mutability until she has exhausted every one of those weapons of guile and statecraft with which the centuries have filled to repletion her vast arsenal. So for nineteen centuries has she always acted when confronted with danger and threatened with disaster; she will not act otherwise when faced with the present crisis, the crisis of the twentieth century. As, therefore, Oscar Wilde well said, that a map of the world which omits Utopia is a map that is incomplete, so any account of the Western world to-day in crisis which omits the Papacy as an essential factor, is also incomplete, and indeed, distorted in character. In the ranks of the adversaries of human progress the Papacy is no mere relic or mediæval survival. It still stands in the foremost rank ; it is still far from the least and not far from the most dangerous of those reactionary and inimical forces which stand between the human race and the ideal of its finest spirits, a civilization completely rational ; that ideal which different ages have differently expressed, but in which all alike of the finest human thinkers have imagined the *summum bonum*—the heart's desire of human aspirations and of human destiny.

In the following pages, the role of the Papacy is examined particularly in relation to the crisis amid which we live, the crisis that to-day threatens to submerge our world, the crisis of the twentieth century. As a still living and still active political force, as a great power, so to speak, and one at that which cherishes and seeks to revive in our modern world the memories of a yet more august past in which her word was law and her writ supreme, the Roman Catholic Church and its papal chief confront this crisis, as so often before they have confronted the successive crises of the past. *Semper eadem*—" For ever the same ". Confident in this unchanging motto, which accurately reflects the remarkable political stability that the Church inherits, if not from heaven, at least from the Rome of the Cæsars, the Catholic Church confronts the world to-day, as she has so often confronted it in previous ages, no less resolved to prevail than of old.

It is, then, the Papacy in relation to the crisis of the twentieth century, in relation not to the past but to the present, that the ensuing pages propose to study. But since the Papacy is an institution in no sense original, but grounded in every thought and action in the past and in the practice thence bequeathed, it is relevant and, indeed, absolutely necessary to discuss first of all the successive relations of the Papacy to the similarly deep crises that have marked its earlier phases.

Five such crises present themselves to the historically informed enquirer, and the first part of this study is occupied with a brief outline of their essential character and of the method which the Roman Church adopted for the purpose of effecting its deliverance from them. It will be found on examination that the Papacy, itself an institution of a compound nature, appertaining concurrently to the political, the religious and the cultural worlds, has never hesitated, when the occasion required, to call upon weapons drawn from each or all of these varying provinces of human activity. But the result, in each of these five successive crises, has been victory, complete or at least partial. In no case has the crisis proved fatal to the papal chair, or to the church and creed of Rome, however dire the disasters that threatened them.

Accordingly, the first part of this book traces these five crises and the modes of deliverance to which the Papacy had recourse in them. These crises of bygone centuries were respectively (1) The fall of the Roman Empire and the migration of the Barbarian nations : (2) The mediæval conflict between the Papacy and the Mohammedan world in the eleventh, twelfth and thirteenth centuries : (3) The renaissance of free thought and secular culture under the ægis of the Arabs and Moors in the thirteenth century : (4) The Protestant Reformation of the sixteenth century : (5) The crisis of modern liberalism that dates from the French Revolution and from the " enlightenment " which preceded it. For the sake of convenience, first the crisis, and then the Papal answer to the crisis, is presented in each case, the whole taking up the first part of this book.

The second and third parts are concerned with the present crisis, that of the twentieth century, the sixth crisis in the history of the Papacy, according to the computation here adopted, and with its antidote, the alliance of Catholicism, ecclesiastical mediævalism, with Fascism, political and cultural mediævalism. Both the present crisis and its future solution, or the attempt at its solution, are presented in broad perspective and without great multiplication of details. We should, indeed, need an entire library even to touch upon all the details which either that crisis or its solution involve.

In fact, large as the crisis of the twentieth century naturally looms in the eyes of the present generation, which is contemporary with it, and seems destined to endure its ravages, yet in the eyes of the Papacy, and in its profound collective memory, it is probable that it takes a more modest place in the wider landscape that memories so tenacious, so ancient, and so various, are bound to disclose. The crisis of a civilization, and even its dire and total collapse, are no new experiences in the annals of an institution which has preceded, and has survived, so many states, and so many once fashionable philosophies of history. With nineteen centuries of history and of crisis behind it, it is unlikely that the crisis of the twentieth century seems as important in the eyes of the Vatican as it does in those of the century itself.

In conclusion, we seek to cast an enquiring glance into the dense murk which hangs, now more than ever, over the future, and to estimate—in so far as circumstantial evidence may be found to offer any `enlightenment—whether in the changed circumstances of the present century, so remote in many respects from those of bygone ages, the Roman See may hope to win its way out of its encircling dangers yet again, and, if so, what results to the human race and human civilization, and also to their mutual alliance, will the Papal-Fascist victory achieve ; or, to use the expression of Bismarck : Is European civilization once more destined to go to Canossa ? [1]

To conclude ; the author would emphasize that he is no theologian or professed critic of theology who seeks to pour fresh light—if, indeed that is possible—upon the origin and nature, human or divine, of the Papal Chair and of the " Roman and Catholic " Church. The present study has no such grandiose and transcendental aim. This book presents a study of human history, primarily of present-day history, and of that of the past only so far as is necessary to throw indispensable

---

[1] See also chapter 2, part one.

light upon the present. The Papacy is here presented as a concrete body with a known past and a doubtful future ; as one of the major forces that operate in present-day history, and as one which, in accordance with human nature and its own past, will strive to survive and even to extend the area of its influence.

While, indeed, it is hotly disputed whether the Papacy does, or does not, give effect to the laws of God, a glance at its history will suffice to disclose that it has always given effective heed to that urge to survival and self-preservation which is nature's first law. Only, Lamarckian rather than Darwinian in this respect, it strives to secure its survival by cunning adaptability and by intelligent foresight, rather than by the unaided power of evolutionary forces to achieve the end of its survival. For, whatever it may say, if one thing can be asserted confidently of the Roman Catholic Church, it is that never at any time has it trusted in the unaided power of truth to prevail !

To-day, as so often in the past, the Roman See is confronted with a crisis from which it seeks to escape. How it seeks to escape, what precedents offer themselves for study and imitation in like case, from what particular perils it desires delivery, by what manipulation of the contemporary chessboard it seeks deliverance, and with what results to humanity and to human progress and civilization—these are the problems with which *The Papacy and Fascism* seeks to deal, the questions which it will strive to answer. There is no more important, fascinating or neglected problem in contemporary history than that afforded by the spectacle of the most ancient and crafty of human institutions pitting its vast experience against the tangled problems of an age so utterly unlike and remote from the ages wherein it was born and grew to maturity. Such is the contemporary drama with which the present study will deal.

NOTE

It should be emphasized that the following pages deal exclusively with the official policy of the Roman Catholic Church, as expressed in the Hierarchy, and, above all, in the Papacy : these organizations are virtually identical with the Church, by reason of the Infallibility Decree, as shown in the first part of the present work. It is not sought to make individual Catholics responsible for the official policy of the church, or vice versa. There are, no doubt, many sincere Catholics, particularly in countries which still retain a democratic tradition, who do not see eye to eye with the pro-Fascist and atavistic policy which their Church has pursued since the Great War under the particular direction of the present Pope, Pius XI, and his reactionary secretary of state, Cardinal Pacelli. Such views, however, remain the views of private individuals, and have, as such, no bearing on the essential thesis of this work.

It may also be added that the relations of the Vatican and the Hitler-state have notably worsened since the following lines were written. This, however, only implies that the decline in revolutionary militancy among the advanced workers, consequent upon the adoption of a policy of compromise by Soviet Russia and the Communist International has sharpened the inherent antagonism between the two Totalitarian States, by weakening their essential bond, the fear of their common enemy and potential " grave-digger ", the international working-class and international socialism.

It cannot be repeated too often or with too much emphasis that the relations at any time existent between the two greatest reactionary forces of our epoch, Fascism and the Roman Catholic Church, depend in final analysis, on the strength or weakness of the international movement of revolutionary socialism. In view of the headlong pace of modern evolution, a twentieth-century version of Bismark's " Kulturkampf " is highly improbable. Even now, one cannot help being struck by the vagueness and mildness of the Papal denunciations of Nazi-ism in the recent encyclical on the German question (March 14, 1937), when compared with the ferocious and full-blooded denunciations that, at every conceivable opportunity, are hurled at the doctrines of the Left parties, and in particular at Communism.

Hence, it is a reasonably safe presumption that, however bitter are the quarrels over jurisdiction and world philosophy that may from time to time divide the two Totalitarian States, yet, in the concrete circumstances of the twentieth century they can never fight out their quarrel to a finish until the common enemy of both is disposed of. At the first movement of the working-class towards its

revolutionary goal, at the first mention of international socialism, the enemies of to-day will bury
the hatchet. Fascism and Catholicism will recognize that, in an age of World Revolution, they
are spiritual twins. Hitler and the Pope, the
" Leader " and the " Holy Father ", will unite in
defence of that which is common to them both,
the destruction of human reason, the denial of
progress, and the mental, moral, and economic
enslavement of mankind.

PART ONE

THE FIVE SUCCESSIVE CRISES
OF THE PAPACY

FIRST CRISIS

THE FALL OF THE ROMAN EMPIRE AND THE MIGRATION OF THE NATIONS

(a) *THE CRISIS*

THE Church of Rome, whether founded by St Peter or not, dates from the first century of the Christian era, and is thus the oldest of existing institutions, with the possible exception of the similarly unbroken dynasty of the Japanese Mikados.[1] No European institution, at any rate, approaches it in longevity. The dogmatic fiction of fully matured Romanism ascribed its foundation to St Peter, and to his successors in perpetuity a monarchical authority, not merely over the Roman Church, but over the Universal (Catholic) Church of Christ.

However, since the democratic character which we now know to have characterized the early Christian communities is quite irreconcilable with such an original monarchical absolutism, it seems probable that the alleged commission of Christ to Peter is a fiction, which most likely was deliberately inserted by some scheming Canonist into the New Testament, as used in the Church

---

[1] See Note A, page 33-34.

of Rome and thence spread, in an uncritical age, to the other Christian Churches.

That the famous phrase on which the Roman See bases its pretensions : " Thou art Peter, and upon this rock I will build my church, and the gates of hell shall not prevail against it ; and I will give unto thee the keys of the kingdom of heaven : and whatsoever thou shalt bind on earth shall be bound in heaven : whatsoever thou shalt loose on earth shall be loosed in heaven ",[1] is a relatively late forgery, unknown to the primitive Christian Church, is virtually proved by the defiant attitude taken up by St Paul in his Epistle to the Galatians—an epistle almost certainly genuine—in which Paul—who must have known of the Divine election of Peter, if it had ever taken place—treats the " Prince of the Apostles " with open contempt.

The question whether Peter was ever in Rome probably cannot be settled either way, but such evidence as there is would seem to point to the conclusion that Peter was one of the " judaizing " Christians who wished to keep nascent Christianity within the confines of the Jewish Synagogue and the Mosaic Law, a party in the early Church who vehemently opposed the efforts of Paul and his coadjutors to naturalize the Christian religion in the Gentile world, whose most striking and permanently successful achievement was to be the Roman Papacy. If this be so, no one would have been more surprised than St Peter himself at the ironic trick of fate which subsequently installed the Galilean habitué of the Synagogue as the mythical

[1] Matthew xvi. 18, 19.

founder of the most anti-Jewish of Churches ! [1]

It would therefore seem likely that the legend, according to which the Divine origin and authority of the Papacy sprang, like Athene, fully grown into existence, is merely one of those numerous convenient legends—if not deliberate forgeries—which served to justify a *fait accompli* in the mind of a credulous age. If the Roman canonists did not scruple to invent the forged " Donation of Constantine " as an historic explanation of the origin of the Papal States, they were not incapable of inventing an even more august authority for the origin of their institution itself, and of ascribing to a single saying of Christ a system of universal authority which was actually the finished product of a long historic movement. It would, after all, be an anachronism—indeed, almost something of a miracle—if the Papacy, the greatest anti-evolutionist force of the twentieth century, admitted the slow working of natural evolution as an adequate cause for its own origins in the first century !

Actually, all that we know of the early history of the Roman See, and of the Roman Church over which it presided, seems to confirm the evolutionary concept of a slow natural movement, without any violent breaks, and without the intervention, not merely of supernatural causes, but even of any extraordinary human ones. So far were the early Popes—if it be permissible so to style them at so early a date in the history of the Roman Church—from being the autocratic " Vicars of Christ ", the divinely appointed rulers of the

[1] *Cf.* St. Paul's *Epistle to the Galatians* ; E. Renan, *Antichrist* ; Karl Kautsky, *The Foundations of Christianity*.

Universal Church, as in later legend, that their authority seems to have been at first confined within the narrow limits of the Imperial City itself; and even within these exiguous bounds it is uncertain how far that authority extended.

It would seem probable, from the few documents available, that the Church of Rome, like the contemporary Churches to whom St Paul addressed his epistles, was originally a democratic institution, in its type of organization rather Presbyterian than Catholic, to anticipate a modern parallel; and that in such a Church the powers of a bishop—if, indeed, the early Popes can be accurately called bishops at all—were extremely limited.

The earliest "successors of Peter", Linus, Clement, etc., are, in any case, such shadowy figures that the little which can be inferred from their evident insignificance argues that they played a very modest rôle. It is no doubt a trifle ironic to suppose that the early " Vicar of Christ " had, in reality, a status approximating to that of the Moderator of a modern Presbyterian Church assembly; but history is full of ironies, and such was probably the fact.[1]

Not merely, did the Papacy owe its rise to the slow processes of natural evolution rather than to an immediate Divine decree, but we miss altogether the real character of its formative period if we fail to add that, during the whole of this era, the first four centuries of its existence, the evolution of the Papacy was a dependent, a contingent evolution. It grew up under the shadow of

[1] *Cf.* Clement, *Epistle to the Corinthians*; Karl Kautsky, *Foundations of Christianity*.

the Roman Empire of the Cæsars, and evolved alongside of that Empire. It was not, in fact, until the middle of the fifth century that a Pope, Leo the Great, ventured, *vis à vis* the barbarian invaders, the Huns of Attila and the Vandals of Genseric, to take any independent action on his own volition.

It is evident to anyone who can penetrate through fictions—inspired and otherwise—and see down to the bedrock of fact that as far as the real historic founder of the Papacy can be said to be any single man, it was Augustus, the founder of the Roman Empire, and not Peter, the obscure fisherman of Galilee. It was the fact that Rome was the capital of the Western World during the first four centuries of its existence, that laid the foundations of Papal Rome so as to prepare her for her grandiose rôle in the mediæval era. Had Augustus, and not Constantine, founded Constantinople to be the capital of the Roman Empire, the Roman See would probably never have emerged from the ruck of provincial institutions.

Not merely was the Roman Church, as Cardinal Newman was later to declare, the " residuary legatee " of the Roman Empire, but prior to obtaining the administration of the estate, it had been the ward of the Empire for four centuries. Christian Rome grew up under the shadow of Pagan Rome. Not only was Papal Rome modelled on Imperial Rome, but the gradual evolution of the democratic State of Republican Rome into the theocratic despotism of the later Roman Cæsars no doubt furnished a direct proto-type for the evolution of the original Roman Presbytery into the monarchical Papacy of later times.

Since the Roman Church, the self-styled " pilgrim of eternity ", considers that it has unlimited time before it, its evolution has been correspondingly slower than was that of its secular Roman model. Whereas only three centuries separated the Byzantine theocracy inaugurated by Diocletian and Constantine at the end of the third century from the genial Republican president, Augustus, eighteen centuries were to elapse before the obscure presbyter of the Catacombs, the first Vicar of Christ, shed all traces of his humble human origin, and proclaimed himself the Infallible Mediator between God and Man, the unerring mouthpiece of Divine Providence, in 1870.

Before this dazzling pinnacle of power could be reached, however, a long evolution had to be undergone by the Papacy ; and as a first and indispensable prelude to this evolution the bishops of Rome had to cut the umbilical cord which bound them in inseparable dependence to their original protector, the Roman Empire, which, however much it may have persecuted them in its Pagan days before Constantine, was nevertheless the necessary guardian of their immature adolescence. The Papacy in Rome could not spread its wings freely for an Imperial flight while situated so close to the Imperial Palace.

Thus it was that, when once the period of its youth was over, the Papacy needed the collapse of the Roman Empire, its erstwhile guardian, as much as it had formerly needed its protection. Its period of incubation was over by the fifth century, and it required a surgical operation to deliver it from the oppressive environment of decaying antiquity. As its own power was still unequal to this task, it was necessary that the Empire of the Roman Cæsars should be shattered by other hands.

This necessary fall of the Roman Empire, which paved the way for Papal supremacy in the West, was achieved in the fifth century by the migration of the German nations, who shattered the Empire in Western Europe and threatened to engulf its institutions in a sea of barbarism. Among the institutions which were at first threatened by the German invaders with destruction was the Papacy, along with the City of Rome itself.

While the Teutonic Migrations constituted, in the broad perspective of general history, a blessing to the nascent Papacy, which thus obtained space for bolder flights than were possible in the cramped atmosphere that the Imperial despotism alone afforded, yet they seemed at first a blessing very effectually disguised. At first, indeed, it seemed that the Papacy would collapse together with the Western Empire in a common ruin, in which all the institutions of the ancient world would be involved. The fall of the Roman Empire represented, accordingly, the first crisis with which the Papacy was confronted. It must solve this crisis or perish. It did solve it. It tamed the barbarians, survived the ancient world, and transformed the age of barbarism into the age of Faith.

Note A : The Mikados

According to the traditional computation, the origin of the dynasty of the Japanese Mikados can be traced back to the seventh century B.C. It is now, however, held that the first Mikado flourished about the beginning of the Christian era, and was thus contemporary with the origin of the Papacy. It may be added that, as an affective historical institution, the Japanese Imperial dynasty cannot be compared with the Papacy, either in the range of its influence or in its duration of actual existence. For most of its history the Japanese Empire has been ruled by Mayors of the Palace —Shoguns—and not by the nominal Emperors.

(b) THE SOLUTION

From the middle of the third century, when they killed the Emperor Decius in battle, the German tribes had been pressing south towards the fertile basin of the Mediterranean. At the opening of the fifth century the foundations of the Western half of the Roman Empire gave way, and from 410 onwards, when the Goths under Alaric sacked Rome, the German nomads occupied successively each of the imperial provinces in the West.

To indicate adequately the causes of the decline and fall of the Roman Empire falls outside the scope of the present work. But we may remark that it would be truer to say that the Empire fell through the operation of its own inherent causes of internal decay than that it was actually conquered by the diminutive tribes of forest nomads who assailed it. As long as it retained its vitality unimpaired, the Empire was fully capable of repelling the barbarians beyond its borders. It was only when enfeebled by the prolonged economic exhaustion which a system of slave economy inevitably engenders, and by the decadent military despotism which was its political counterpart, that the Roman Empire finally lost the strength to continue a successful resistance to the barbarians in the West. In the East, where its resources were greater, the Byzantine Empire continued, albeit with reduced power and territory, for another millennium before it completely succumbed to the Western expansion, the *Drang nach Westen*, of the Ottoman Turks (1453).

The effects of the collapse of the Western Empire on the fortunes both of Christianity and of the Papacy were of necessity profound. The appalling misery which characterized the last stages of that Empire was directly favourable to the growth of religious feeling in an age in which very obviously " fear engendered religious belief ". With the decay of the Roman Empire owing to the utter exhaustion of the Italian provinces by a wholesale and ruthless system of agricultural slavery and amid unparalleled political and physical disasters, despair fell upon all, and upon none more than the wretched slaves. Despair and disaster drove men to religion for consolation, while, as Professor Seeley aptly states : " the age was religious because it was an age of servitude." The hopelessness of this world encouraged an aspiration for a world to come, and this provided the motive and helped to determine the form of the religious revival.

In such circumstances, in an age that had lost all faith in the possibility of social amelioration in this life, the religion that rose to chief place could only be the religion of the subject and the slave ;

so Christianity, with its cardinal ethic of submission —" Slaves, obey your masters "—was an eminently suitable creed for such times. Moreover, the very fact that it claimed to be universal or catholic marked it out as the natural successor of the universal Empire, Rome, the first example of political " catholicism "—if the phrase be allowable —in European history. This fact operated directly in favour of the Bishops of Rome, the Popes—who appeared before the barbarians as the representatives and lineal successors of the vanished Roman Emperors, whose civilization and political administration, so incomparably superior to their own, continued to exercise a perennial fascination on the German kinglets who reigned over the former Roman provinces throughout the Dark Age that followed upon the demise of the Empire.

Indeed, if Western Europe did not relapse entirely into barbarism at this epoch, this was due largely to the profound influence of the traditions of Roman world-power which still subsisted, and the Bishop of Rome, by his position at the traditional heart of this empire, came to be looked upon as its spiritual head. His position, indeed, had become definitely monarchical within the Church, and the Lombard conquest in the latter half of the sixth century, by confining the power of the Byzantine (Eastern) Empire to a narrow strip of territory round Ravenna, threw the Papacy on its own resources, by freeing it from the yoke of Constantinople, and concentrating the temporal rule of the City of Rome and the lands immediately adjacent in the hands of the Pope, thus laying the foundations of the temporal power of the Papacy.

The situation of the Papacy, from the fifth to the ninth century, may thus be summarized : its position as ruler of the impoverished Rome of the Dark Ages was too weak to guarantee physical immunity, let alone any dominant rôle in the affairs of the contemporary world. To secure its continued existence as an autonomous power, the Papacy had to evolve sufficient temporal (*i.e.* political) power to ensure its existence in the stormy world of the Dark Ages. Whatever may have been the defects of the idea that underlay the Temporal Power, if and when considered from a purely religious standpoint, some degree of political independence was a necessity to the Papacy, if it was to endure in that age of iron. For the Popes to retain the respect of the surrounding barbarians, it was absolutely essential that they should be freed from subjection to them.

Thus, the first and most indispensable condition for survival in the crisis that had engulfed the Roman world was the creation of an independent Papal State, immune from barbarian invasion. Without such a safeguard, the Papacy could hardly have existed. This once secured, it was necessary for its assumption of an international rôle that the German barbarians should be converted to Christianity, *and that by the Roman See and not by anyone else.*

This latter condition was indispensable likewise because neither the Arian (unitarian) Creed which several German tribes—Visigoths, Vandals, etc., had embraced, nor that type of Christianity propagated throughout Northern Europe by Irish monks, acknowledged the authority of the Papacy. It is

thus evident that the two essential prerequisites
for a solution of its first crisis were, for the Papacy,
the creation of an independent Papal state, and the
conversion of Europe to Roman Catholicism and
to obedience to the Papal See as head of the Western
Church.   Such were the problems which the age
presented for solution.   Between the years 500 and
800, these problems were solved; the Papacy
emerged from a world in ruins, and emerged
stronger than it went in, no longer a local Italian
bishopric, but an international force and a
European power.

The problem of temporal power was solved by
a combination of legal trickery and bold diplomacy.
The forged " Donation of Constantine " (late
eighth century) deceived an ignorant and credulous
age with its bold assumption that the temporal
dominion over the city and province of Rome
was a legacy from the first Christian Emperor,
and even that he had left Rome for Constantinople
in order to make way for the temporal power;
a very convenient reading of history from the
Papal point of view.   Later, when the Italian
Lombards, the last of the barbarian immigrants to
dismember the former Roman Empire (second
half of the sixth century) proved troublesome
neighbours to the newly formed Papal states,
the Popes invented a diplomatic " balance of
power ", and called in the Frankish kings, already
converted from paganism to Catholicism, to act
as the protectors of the Roman See from its Lombard
neighbours.

This line of policy ended in the formation of an
alliance between the two strongest powers in

Western Europe—the Roman Popes, whose organization now represented what was left of Roman civilization, and the Frankish kings, who by the end of the eighth century had become the most powerful rulers in what was left of a Christendom sorely diminished by the Arab invasions of the preceding century. The advantages of this alliance were mutual. The Frankish kings, and in particular Charlemagne, the ablest and most powerful of them, proved capable of safeguarding the Popes from troublesome neighbours and of preserving the nascent Papal states, while the establishment of the Roman Church as a temporal power, indissolubly associated with the traditions of Rome, caused it to be eagerly sought as an ally by the Frankish aspirants to the throne of a revived Roman Empire.

The alliance was solemnly celebrated on Christmas Day 800, when the Pope crowned Charlemagne as " Roman " Emperor, thus bringing into existence the mediæval or Catholic Empire, the " Holy " Roman Empire, to distinguish the Christian Empire from its predecessor, whose traditions were Pagan rather than Christian. A modern historian has trenchantly summed up the net result of this alliance upon European civilization :

> " In the name of Christianity Charles the Great rolled back the tide of Saracen invasion from the Pyrenees, and established the foundations of Christendom."[1]

Meanwhile, concurrently with the establishment of the temporal power of the Papacy, the work of

[1] Prof. Jenks, *Short History of Politics.*

converting the barbarians from Paganism, or heresy, was carried on by Rome with conspicuous vigour. In the accomplishment of this task the Popes found another invaluable ally in the newly-founded Benedictine Order, by whose agency the power of the Papacy, and also the relics of the old Roman civilization which it preserved, were spread beyond the confines of Italy among the peasant and semi-barbaric states which now divided Europe.

The Benedictine Order, founded by St Benedict (*c*, 480-550) carried the Papal civilization to the barbarians beyond the Alps.   Under its auspices Boniface converted the Germans, and Augustine —sent directly to England by the Benedictine Pope Gregory the Great—converted Kent, the first seat of Anglo-Saxon Christianity, whence it subsequently spread to the rest of the Anglo-Saxon Heptarchy, where, after a keen ecclesiastical competition, the Roman form of Christianity prevailed over its schismatic competitor, Irish or Celtic Christianity.[1] The founder of the " black monks " St Benedict, was himself a Roman aristocrat of the Anician *gens*, the only senatorial family which could trace back its lineage to republican days, and his monks appeared among the barbarians not merely as Christian missionaries, but as the emissaries and torchbearers of a new Roman civilization which now looked to Papal, instead of to Imperial, Rome as its centre.   Alongside of the Roman Catholic faith and the Papal supremacy, the monks carried the seeds of the political and economic system of ancient Rome, and under their ægis the Dark Ages began to give way to the

[1] See Note B, page 43.

Christian civilization of the Middle Ages, whose centre was Papal Rome.

The conversion of the semi-barbaric kinglets of the contemporary Anglo-Saxon states of the period of the " Heptarchy " (*i.e.* the seven " kingdoms " into which England was then divided) was typical of this work of religious and cultural enlightenment, which marked the expansion of the influence of Papal Rome among the ultramontane barbarians, and may serve as an example of the rise of the new Catholic civilization in other parts of Europe.

In Saxon England the establishment of political society was closely followed by the replacement of the older tribal religious cults by Christianity. The rule of the king and of his warrior-band over the agricultural settlements of the tribes undermined patriarchalism and weakened its religious reflex.

Consequently, the conversion of Ethelbert of Kent to Christianity was the signal for the conversion of England. The new religion spread from court to court of the Heptarchy, aiding the developing kingship in its conflict with the traditional forms of archaic tribal society, and introducing a model of political organization that was the ripened fruit of Roman political experience. It was natural that barbarians who had now outgrown the nomadic society of the primeval forest should also outgrow the primitive nature cults, such as those of the old Teutonic gods, Odin, Thor and Freya, which represented the religious reactions of primitive tribal life.

As the German tribes who conquered, or rather

occupied, the Roman Empire, rose above the level, of the forest, they came within the framework of cultural and juridical organization, to which the dogmas and ethics of Catholic Christianity corresponded. The "nations" who migrated from the barbaric North to the Mediterranean similarly migrated from Wotan to Christ. As the Roman Church alone remained of the institutions of the vanished world of civilized antiquity, adherence to it was the equivalent of the adoption of civilization by the barbarians as they rose above the primitive level. At the same time the Catholic provincials "permeated" those of their barbaric conquerors who had adopted Christianity in a heretical or schismatic form.[1]

The actual result of the policy of the Popes between the first and the ninth centuries was to secure their independence by the creation of the independent "patrimony of Peter"—*i.e.*, the germ of the later Papal States—and by the creation of the Holy Roman Empire as their political protector. At the same time, by the agency of the Benedictine missionaries and their confrères, the Papacy extended its jurisdiction, both fiscal and spiritual, over Teutonic Europe. Hence, in place of the secular classical civilization of Europe there arose the outline of the new spiritual civilization of Europe, which again centred upon Rome. The Papacy emerged from its first crisis not only intact, but a Transalpine and European Power. From a local Roman bishopric it became an Empire, European in fact, and universal in theory, precisely as Imperial Rome had been before it. The

[1] See Note C, page 44.

Popes of Rome succeeded the Cæsars as the rulers of the West. Their Empire, as yet chiefly spiritual, followed the lines of the Western Empire, and was bounded by the schismatic Greeks and the Mohammedan infidels to the East, and by the Ocean to the West. Not merely had it survived the barbarian flood, but it had guided the impetuous current towards the Tiber.

Note B : Irish Christianity

Ireland had never formed part of the Roman Empire ; consequently it never formed part of the area in which Græco-Roman civilization prevailed. It was converted in the fifth century by the British missionary, St Patrick, and developed a type of Christianity suitable to Celtic tribal life, monastic rather than episcopal in character, and independent of the Papal See. From the island monasteries of Iona and Lindisfarne Irish monks converted Northern England (Northumbria) to the Celtic (schismatic) version of the new faith. For a time, Anglo-Saxon England was divided between the Roman and the Irish rites. Eventually, however, the superior organization of the Roman Church, so essential in a society as chaotic as was that of the Heptarchy, weighted the scales on behalf of Rome. The final decision in favour of the Papal Church was made at the Synod of Whitby, in 664 when Northumbria deserted Iona for Rome. Ireland, however, remained outside the Roman Communion until the late Middle Ages. " The Isle of the Saints " had a long ecclesiastical history before it became the Isle of the Popes.

Note C : *Arianism among the Teutonic Tribes*

Among the original invaders of the Roman Empire, three peoples, the Ostrogoths, the Visigoths and the Vandals, had been Arian, or Unitarian—to cut out fine theological quibbles—from the start. The Ostrogoths and Vandals had been obliterated by the Byzantine armies of Justinian in the sixth century, when the Emperor made his grandiose effort to reconquer the lost Western provinces of the Roman Empire. The Visigoths were converted to Catholicism, in 589. In the case of all these Teutonic tribes it was the value of the church organization to the royal power which decided the issue in favour of Rome.

" Christianity well repaid the favour of princes ; under the cry of ' one Church and one King ' the older tribal divisions were ultimately wiped out, and England became one nation with Church and State in intimate alliance. The intimate connection between the King and the Church was the best possible safeguard against any revival of patriarchalism in connection with ancestor worship." [1]

The Roman Church, in short, furnished the only possible nucleus for an organized administration in kingdoms that felt the need for a settled government, but had no educated lay class available for the indispensable duties of a bureaucracy.

[1] Edward Jenks, *Short History of Politics*.

Chapter II

SECOND CRISIS

THE CONFLICT WITH ISLAM

(a) *THE CRISIS*

THE Papacy had called in Charlemagne and his Franks to safeguard its metropolis and its independence against the local barbarians, the Lombards. After the death of the great Emperor in 814, his Empire quickly decomposed when once the strong hand of the Emperor was removed, and Europe sank into a welter of bloodshed and social chaos. In addition to the prevailing confusion, new enemies burst upon the newly-established Christendom and assailed it from every side. The Vikings, or Norsemen, attacked it from the sea, the newly arrived Magyars (Hungarians) from the East, and the Arabs, crusaders of Islam, fell upon it simultaneously by land and sea, in Spain, France, and on the coasts of the Mediterranean. For two terrible centuries—*c.* 814-1000—an age of iron laid hold of Western Europe, an age which synchronized with the degradation of the Papacy itself to the nadir of spiritual, moral and political decadence.

A German historian thus vividly describes the chaos which ensued :

" The collapse of the Roman Empire set in motion not only the Teutons, but also all the numerous apparently inexhaustible tribes of semi-barbarians in the neighbourhood. As the Teutons moved towards the West and South, other peoples pressed upon them. The Slavs crossed the Elbe; from the steppes of South Russia came one Cossack tribe after another, as well as Huns, Avars, and Hungarians, who extended their plundering expeditions along the unprotected Danube, and even beyond the Black Forest and the Rhine, and beyond the Elbe to Northern Italy. From Scandinavia, too, expeditions of Norman pirates followed one another. No sea was too broad for them to traverse, no Empire too large to attack. They ruled the Baltic, seized Russia, established themselves in Iceland, discovered America long before Columbus, but what for us is important, from the end of the eighth to the twelfth century they threatened to destroy the whole laboriously constructed civilization of the settled Teutonic tribes. They soon attacked the Spaniards, and finally extended their raids as far as Southern France and Italy.

" The most dangerous enemy of the settled Teutonic tribes was, however, the Arabs, or, rather, the Saracens, as the writers of the Middle Ages called all those eastern peoples set in motion by the Arabs to seek booty and a habitat in more highly civilized countries.

" In the year 638 the Arabs invaded Egypt, and quickly conquered the whole of the northern coast of Africa; they appeared at the beginning of the eighth century in Spain, and not quite a hundred years after they invaded Egypt, they threatened France. Charles Martel's victory near

Tours saved France from the fate of the Empire of the western Goths ; but the Saracens were by no means rendered powerless. They stayed in Spain, established themselves in North Italy and in Southern France, occupied the most important Alpine paths, and sallied forth to raid the northern slopes of the Alps.

"During the migration of the peoples the settled Teutonic tribes had occupied the greater part of Europe and a part of North Africa ; now they saw themselves confined to a small space and were hardly able to maintain this. Burgundy, which was practically the geographical centre of the Catholic West in the tenth century, was as much exposed to the invasion of the Normans as to the Hungarians and Saracens. The end of the peoples of Western Christendom seemed at hand." [1]

It is unnecessary to add to the lucid analysis quoted above, particularly as the features it describes are, in the main, identical with those of the earlier influx of the Teutonic tribes within the boundaries of the Roman Empire, which marked the first crisis of the Papacy already described. The only new feature was the inroads of the fanatical Arab crusaders of Islam, who penetrated much further into the West than any previous Oriental invader had done. For the Papacy to surmount the second crisis in its history which threatened it with physical destruction—when, in 846, the Saracens actually occupied the suburbs of Rome itself—it was necessary for it to tighten its authority over what

[1] Karl Kautsky, *Thomas More and his Utopia*, pp. 43-4.

was left of the Catholic Empire, and to convert
or drive back by armed force the various invaders
of Christendom. From this crisis, as from the
preceding one, the Papacy found way of escape
—a way which not merely enabled it to emerge
from the ruins of its contemporary world, but
actually extended the area of its authority and
enhanced its power and prestige.

(b) THE SOLUTION

During the tenth century the Papacy sank to
the lowest depth of degradation. During this
period Papal authority was set at nought in the
City of Rome itself, where the citizens frequently
rose in revolt against their bishops. Moreover,
infamous associations with licentious women made
the Papacy an object of contempt, and gave rise
to the legend of " Pope Joan "—the female Pope
—which dates from the era under discussion.
While, in its final form, the legend is unhistorical,
yet several of the Papal concubines of this period
actually attained to positions of such great influence as to become virtual Pope-makers, and
seated their sons and lovers on the Chair of St
Peter.

The external weakness of the Roman See during
this terrible period, when Catholic Europe was
assailed simultaneously by a renewal of the barbarian invasions and by the new danger represented
by the rival religion of Islam, was matched by its
internal weakness. As in the fifth century, so also
in the tenth, a shrewd and well-informed observer

would probably have predicted the early collapse of the Papacy.

Nothing, however, is more remarkable in the history of that extraordinary institution than its power to survive and transcend the individuals who successively embodied it. The Papacy has, in fact, always been of greater importance than the Popes ! In the eleventh century, when seemingly at death's door, it staged a remarkable revival and triumphantly solved the problems which then faced it.

Beginning with the learned Pope Sylvester II, the pupil of Arab science (999-1002), and ending with the great Hildebrand—Pope Gregory VII (1072-85), probably the greatest member of the long line of Popes, the Papacy achieved simultaneously a moral reformation and a political and military triumph over the enemies of Christendom and of the Roman supremacy therein. In this memorable transformation, the Counter-Reformation of the eleventh century, the initiative again came from the Benedictine Order, whose monastery at Cluny in France was the spiritual centre of this ecclesiastical revival.

From the point of view of the internal re-organization of the Church, the Papal reformation was chiefly noticeable for the sharp division which it introduced between the clergy and the laity, a distinction foreign to the early Church, but necessary for the transformation of the clergy into an international gendarmerie, " the Papal Militia ". From that time on, the transformation of the Roman Catholic Church into a corporation of priests proceeded uninterruptedly until it reached its consummation at the Council of Trent. The transference of the right of Papal election from the original electors, the people of Rome, to the College of Cardinals, which was made in 1059 by Nicholas II and Hildebrand (then archdeacon of Rome), marked another important step in this transformation. Like many other things in Catholic practice and dogma, it is probable that this centralization of the Church, and the ecclesiastical celibacy which formed part of the means for securing it, while later a source of weakness, were instrumental in effecting a moral reformation in the eleventh century.

The real crisis, however, was political and military rather than moral in character. Unless the Arabs and the Viking pirates could be converted or driven back, the question would still remain one of the revival, and not of the reformation, of Catholic Christendom and the Papal power. The question of the internal position of the Popes in Christendom depended ultimately, therefore, upon their success in solving the external problem.

How the eleventh century Papacy brilliantly accomplished this task, first winning over to its side one section of its enemies and then utilizing them as allies in its conflict with the other, in a word, hurling the Northern enemy against the Southern one, is thus described by Kautsky in a masterly passage :

" And just when the pressure of external foes was most severe, the political power was most impotent, the feudal anarchy was most unchecked, and the only firm, coherent power was the Papal Church.

"Like the monarchical powers, the Papal power, in its contest with the external enemy, became strong enough to defy its foes at home.

"The Saracens, who were to some extent superior in culture, could only be grappled with by the sword; in the fight with Islam the Papacy summoned and organized the whole of Christendom. The unstable enemies in the North and the East could be temporarily repulsed by force of arms, but not permanently subdued. They were subjugated by the same means as the Roman Church had employed to subjugate the Teutons; they were forced to adopt a higher mode of production—after being won for Christianity, they settled down and were rendered harmless.

"The Papacy celebrated a brilliant triumph over the Normans. It transformed them from the most formidable of the Northern enemies of Christianity into the most pugnacious and energetic antagonists of the Southern enemy. The Papacy made an alliance with the Normans similar to that which it had formerly concluded with the Franks. The alliance recognized the fact that the Normans had not been pacified by their incorporation in the feudal mode of production. They remained a restless, predatory people, but the object of their raids was now changed. By being made feudal Lords, the land hunger peculiar to feudalism was aroused in them and from plunderers they became conquerors.

" The Papacy knew how to make excellent use of this appetite for conquest—by turning it against the Saracens. The Papacy had as much to gain from the victory of the Normans as the Normans from the victory of the Papacy. The Normans became vassals of the Pope, who invested them with their conquests as fiefs. The Pope blessed their arms, and the Papal blessing was of great effect in the eleventh century, as it placed the powerful organization of the Church at the service of the recipient. With Papal assistance the Normans became able to conquer England and Lower Italy.[1]

" By enlisting the Normans in its service, the Papacy attained to the summit of its power. It triumphed not only over its internal enemies, it not only imposed on the German Emperor the humiliation of Canossa,[2] it felt strong enough to take the offensive against the Saracens ; the epoch of the Crusades began.

" The Popes were the organizers of the Crusades, the Normans their champions. What drew the latter towards the East was land hunger ; they established feudal States in Palestine, Syria, Asia Minor, Cyprus and finally in the Greek Empire as well. . . . It testifies to the great power of the Papacy that it was able to compel many elements to participate in the Crusades which had nothing to gain thereby. Many German Emperors were obliged, much against

---

[1] The latter then occupied by the Arabs.
[2] See Note D, pages 54-5.

their will, to recruit for the Papal armies and to carry the Papal flag, the Cross." [1]

Thus the eleventh-century Papacy adopted, and triumphed by adopting, the old principle of the Roman Republic : " Divide and rule." It converted Northern and Eastern Europe, thereby enlarging the bounds of Christendom until they became equivalent to Western Europe. Hungary and the Scandinavian countries, Denmark, Norway, Sweden and Iceland, were converted in the eleventh century ; again it was the kings who led the way, as in the case of the earlier Teutonic tribes, viz. " Saint Olaf " of Norway and " Saint Stephen " of Hungary. The Papacy then hurled united Europe against the East, with brilliant, if temporary, results, from the time of the capture of Jerusalem in the First Crusade in 1099.

At the same time as the Arab menace was first put on the defensive, and then broken, the Christian Spaniards, with the active support of the Papacy, began a successful offensive against the Mohammedan rulers of Spain. In 1202 a Norman-Venetian Crusade temporarily reunited the schismatic Greeks to the Catholic obedience by taking Constantinople and breaking up the Byzantine Empire.

As a result of these brilliantly successful policies the Papacy in the eleventh and twelfth centuries was incomparably the most powerful force in

[1] Kautsky, *op. cit.*, pp. 44-46. Throughout this passage Kautsky refers to the converted Northmen—gallicized into " Normans "— who settled in Northern France—Normandy—thence issuing in the eleventh century under William the Conqueror and Robert Guiscard to conquer respectively England, and Naples and Sicily ; in both cases with the active assistance of the Papacy.

Europe, and ruled a domain wider than that of Imperial Rome at its zenith ; and the authority of the Papal monarchy was cultural and political, no less than religious and moral, in character.

Indeed, Europe by the twelfth century had recovered from the Dark Ages, and had evolved a civilization ; but a civilization quite remote in its world outlook from that of Pagan antiquity ; a clerical civilization, in which the clergy were the educated class, theology the " Queen of the Sciences ", and the Pope the ruler. So great, in fact, was his power, that he was able to encroach successfully on the temporal power of the governments, and, in particular, the Roman See inflicted many defeats and humiliations upon its former protector, the Holy Roman Empire, against whose rival power the Papacy waged a bitter, and on the whole a victorious, struggle.

So great was the power of the Papal Monarchy throughout this, its classical, epoch, that it claimed to override the secular authority : the famous doctrine of the " two swords "—the " sword " of the Church independent of, and sharper than, the sword of the State—merely registered the actual state of Christendom. The Papacy had not merely solved its second crisis, but in solving it had attained to undreamed-of heights of power.

Note D : Canossa

In 1077 the Holy Roman Emperor and German King, Henry IV, was forced to desist from his unsuccessful opposition to the Papacy over the question of the investiture of bishops. To obtain relief from the Bull of excommunication and deposition which Pope Gregory VII (Hildebrand) had hurled against him, Henry was forced to cross the Alps in mid-winter and stand in his shirt in freezing cold outside Canossa, the castle of the Pope's ally, Matilda of Tuscany, until the Pope admitted him to make an abject submission. Henceforth Canossa signified the apogee of clerical power in political matters and the corresponding humiliation of secular governments before the ecclesiastical power. It is in this sense that " Canossa " has been used by Bismarck and other modern politicians. —See Parts Two and Three of this book.

THIRD CRISIS

THE RENAISSANCE OF EUROPEAN CIVILIZATION

(a) *THE CRISIS*

THE crisis of the thirteenth century—the third crisis which the Papacy met and surmounted—differed both in origin and results from its predecessors. In the twelfth and thirteenth centuries, civilization, submerged in Western Europe since the fall of the Roman Empire in the fifth century, once more appeared walking without ecclesiastical crutches on its own proper secular feet. Hence, whereas the first two crises of the Papacy already described, were crises of barbarism, that of the thirteenth century, which now claims our attention, was caused not by too little civilization, as was the case with the barbarian invaders, but by too much.

Henceforward, the rôle of the Papacy in European culture was defensive and retrogressive, and it has remained increasingly so down to our own day. For whereas the Roman See was undeniably far more civilized than the illiterate barbarians who overthrew the Roman Empire, and later enjoyed a decided superiority over the semi-civilized German rulers of the eleventh and twelfth centuries, from the thirteenth century onward the clerical civilization represented by the Popes faced a civilization based on human reason. From that time onward, the Papacy lagged farther and farther behind in the march of human progress, and increasingly took on the arch-reactionary lineaments which we know to-day.[1]

In point of fact, the thirteenth century marked a sharp line of division in the historic development of the Papacy. Until then, Europe was still in the stage when any civilization, even a sacerdotal, theocratic one, as was that of the Papacy, was better than the semi-savagery which was the only available alternative. Thenceforward, the choice before Europe was between a real civilization—*i.e.* one grounded upon autonomous human reason and experience—and a sacerdotal culture which could at best be described only as semi-civilized, since its postulates were unverifiable and its criterion was a legendary authority whose claims to credibility were so far from being self-evident that they clashed increasingly with the expanding empire of scientific knowledge.

In a word, whereas, prior to the thirteenth century, the problem of the Papacy was to raise Europe above a level of barbarism to which her doctrines were not adapted, after it her increasingly difficult and pressing problem was to prevent European civilization from advancing beyond the point at which it ceased to be compatible with the Papal claims, and with the Catholic mythology upon which these claims were ostensibly based. Whereas, accordingly, the Papacy resolved the first two crises in its history in a progressive manner, it

[1] See Note E, pp. 62-3.

could, and can to-day, solve the later crises in its history only by checking the natural evolution of European civilization and by opposing to progress the barrier of an energetic reaction. Indeed, since the revival of European secular culture, which dates properly from the thirteenth rather than the sixteenth century, the effective motto of the Roman Church and See in relation to human progress may well be expressed in the words of a modern playwright :

> " For Heaven be thanked ! each new attraction
> Is still attended by—Reaction."[1]

The great epochs of human civilization have generally resulted from the intermixture of cultural forces of diverse origin. The civilization of the Middle Ages formed no exception to this general principle of sociology. The Crusades, promoted by the Papal power itself, proved the indirect cause of the next crisis which threatened its power.

By the twelfth century the Mohammedan peoples had long since shed the primitive manners of the desert which marked the early Crusaders of Islam in the seventh. The primitive vigour of the Arabs, mingling with the ancient cultures of the Near East, had created a new civilization, in some respects superior to any that had preceded it, and certainly far superior to the contemporary rusticity of Europe. Stimulated by a renaissance of Greek, or rather of Hellenistic, science, a great Arab, or more precisely, Arab-Persian civilization had arisen throughout the Mohammedan world, from Samarkand to Spain.

Whether this civilization was or was not one

[1] Ibsen, *Brand*, Act V.

of the great creative civilizations of the world has been hotly disputed; but it is incontestable that it was incomparably superior, on both the mental and material planes, to anything known in contemporary Europe.

The history of civilization has generally recorded a successive oscillation between East and West; and for several centuries prior to the epoch of the Crusades, the general level of civilization in the Orient was as much above that of contemporary Europe as, in later centuries, it was the reverse. It was the contact forcibly established by the Crusades between the barbaric West and the civilized East which marked the beginning of that migration of civilization from East to West which has proceeded uninterruptedly from that time to our own day.[1]

For more than a century and a half—from the end of the eleventh to the middle of the thirteenth —a series of Crusades, in which most of the European potentates took part and whose naval power was furnished by the Italian maritime republics, kept up a continual flow of intercourse between East and West.

The result of this continuous contact with the brilliant civilization which had produced the *Arabian Nights*, the principles of physical science, and the sceptical philosophy of Averroes, Avicenna and Omar Khayyam, was similar to that generally produced on semi-barbarians by the impact of a

---

[1] *Cf.* J. W. Draper, *Conflict of Religion and Science*; Joseph MacCabe, *The Splendour of Moorish Spain*; H. Lammens, *Etudes sur le siécle des Ommayades*. The local variation of the Arab-Persian civilization in Spain is sometimes referred to as "Moorish" from the number of Moors who accompanied the Arabs to Spain.

more advanced culture : a new civilization made its appearance.

In the thirteenth century the first fruits of this new cultural intermixture began to display themselves. The physical invasion of the Crusaders was now answered by an Oriental invasion, the invasion of ideas, an invasion intellectual and spiritual, but no less deadly than one waged with carnal weapons.

By this time, the original monotheistic rigour which had characterized the creed of Islam in its early days had evaporated, and a scientific pantheism had been evolved by the process of philosophical criticism out of the basic Mohammedan conception of the unique existence and unity of God. In the eyes of the intellectual classes, who were the torch-bearers of the new Arab civilization, the rigid lines of the Mohammedan creed of uncompromising monotheism were softened into a " scientific " blur in which the sharp line of demarcation drawn by the Koran between the Creator and the creation has wholly disappeared.

It was in the form of scientific pantheism, indeed of a sceptical agnosticism at least as regards any distinctive divine revelation, that the so-called Mohammedan culture of the East came sweeping down the western sky in the thirteenth century. We say " so-called ", since it is probable that such a creed would have commended itself as little to, and would have been as little approved by, the author of the Koran, the prophet Mohammed himself, as the very similar views of some modern " Christian " theologians would have been approved by the historical fountain-head whence the ocean of Christianity ultimately derives, the historical Jesus of the Synoptic Gospels.

The tide that came flooding in from the East threatened to sweep away each and every belief in those religious dogmas which, hitherto unchallenged since the downfall of Paganism in the fourth century, formed the sheet-anchor of the sacerdotal culture which centred around Papal Rome.

It is probable that in the first half of the thirteenth century the intellect of Europe was as completely lost to the Catholic Church, and had succumbed as completely to the fascinating pantheism of Averroes and his coadjutors, as in later days the intellect of Europe " apostatized " to Voltaire and Diderot, or to Hæckel and Huxley. As the Papal power, and equally the Papal civilization which had sprung up under its leadership, professed to derive their title-deeds from the Christian revelation, and ruled a superstitious generation in the name of that revelation, it was a matter of life and death to the Papacy to suppress this rising tide of unbelief.

The Papacy then, as now, denied historic evolution ; and it had not overcome Odin in the name of Christ, in order to see Christ, in his turn, overcome by Reason. As previously observed, the crisis of the thirteenth century differed wholly from its historic precursors. Then, it was a question of saving Europe from too much barbarism and from a patriarchal nature-worship that represented an earlier stage of religious development than did the Catholic Church and the Christian religion.

Now, the precise opposite was the case ; Europe must be saved from becoming too civilized. It must, in fact, be saved from itself, from the secular consequences of its own natural and rational development. For the achievement of this purpose, a technique of repression, of scientific terrorism, must be evolved. The Papacy now became reactionary ; having raised European barbarism to its own level, it must henceforth forcibly prevent it from advancing further.

Thus it came about that by the inauguration and active conduct of the Catholic terror, by the establishment of organized repression as a permanent element in Christendom and in social relations, the Papacy alone could prevent artificially the resuscitation of the secular civilization of Europe and its return to the secular tradition of civilized antiquity. The Inquisition was the Procrustean bed on which the limbs of European society were henceforth distorted from their proper shape. It was by means of terror, systematic and permanent in character, since the disease of " dangerous thoughts " that it sought to cure also remained henceforth permanently domiciled in Europe, that the Papacy artificially prolonged the Middle Ages and, in so prolonging them, prolonged simultaneously its own life and its own power.

Note E : The Papacy and Reaction

" The Catholic Church achieved, during the Middle Ages, the most organic society and the most harmonious inner synthesis of instinct, mind, and spirit that the Western world has ever known.

St Francis, Thomas Aquinas, and Dante represent its summit as regards individual development. The cathedrals, the mendicant orders, and the triumph of the Papacy over the Empire represent its supreme political success. But the perfection which had been achieved was a narrow perfection ; instinct, mind and spirit all suffered from curtailment in order to fit into the pattern, laymen found themselves subject to the Church in ways which they resented, and the Church used its power for rapacity and oppression. The perfect synthesis was an enemy to new growth, and after the time of Dante all that was living in the world had first to fight for its right to live against the representatives of the old order." Bertrand Russell, *Principles of Social Reconstruction*, p. 199.

(b) *THE SOLUTION*

By the very fact of its widespread influence and of its universal claims the Papacy was involved in a continuous series of actions and reactions. As already remarked, the Papacy had rolled back the tide of Islam by adopting the enemy's own weapon. The " Jihad ", or Holy War, had been ordained by the prophet Mohammed himself as a religious duty, opening the gate of heaven to the believer who fell in battle against the enemies of Islam. It was above all by this device that that consummate politician enrolled the predatory tribes of Arabia under the flag of the new religion. The Papacy adopted the Jihad, and, under its Christian name of " Crusade ", enlisted the cupidity and fanaticism

of the warlike barbarians of Europe against the
world of Islam, with a facility and a success which
recalled and rivalled that with which Mohammed's
successors hurled the warlike barbarians of Asia
against Christendom. Between the armies of Omar
and those of Godfrey de Bouillon there was, indeed,
but little difference ; even the acts of vandalism
ascribed to them are remarkably similar.[1]

Not merely was this the case with regard to the
character of the Crusades, but their results also
were very similar to those which had followed
upon the earlier victories of the Mohammedan
armies. Just as the rude Arabs and Moors had
acquired and renewed the higher civilization of
the Christian and Zoroastrian East, so the Crusaders
brought back the higher material and intellectual
culture which the Mohammedan East had meanwhile acquired.

In both cases the new mixed culture took on a
sceptical or heretical form. The brilliant court of
Damascus, where the Ommeyade Khalifs, the
" successors " of the Puritan prophet Mohammed,
appeared in the pulpit drunk and patronized the
work of free-thinking scientists, was matched by
the equally brilliant court at Palermo, where the
" Holy Roman " Emperor, Frederick Hohenstaufen
(1194-1250) kept an oriental harem, and tacitly
accepted the authorship of the crowning blasphemy
of the Middle Ages, the *De Tribus Impostoribus*,
wherein it was categorically asserted that religion
was invented by rogues for the purpose of fleecing
their dupes, and that Moses, Jesus, and Mohammed,
the " three impostors " *par excellence*, were merely

[1] See Note F, p. 74.

three monuments to the bottomless credulity of the human mind.[1]

The earlier invasions of Islam had already established points of contact between East and West. In the eighth and ninth centuries the Arabs had occupied Spain, Sicily, lower Italy, and Provence. In all these districts they had left physical and cultural traces of their presence.[2] (In Spain they preserved a foothold in Granada down to 1492.) It was, accordingly, along channels already well marked that the flood of oriental ideas came sweeping in the thirteenth century.

While the endemic warfare that raged between Christians and Moors in Spain largely prevented the spread of Mohammedan rationalism across the Pyrenees, the two former provinces of the Arab Empire, Sicily and Provence, became centres of the new anti-clerical civilization. The one became the scene of the most audacious attempt to destroy the mediæval Church; the other, the home of that ubiquitous heresy known as Manicheanism or Dualism, which runs like a refrain through the religious and social underworld of the Middle Ages, and which, but for the ferocious repression directed against it, would probably have come to rank as one of the great religions in human history.[3]

The thirteenth century witnessed one of the most audacious attempts to unite diverse political and cultural forces against a single enemy that European history has ever known. Undoubtedly

---

[1] *Cf*. E. Kantorowicz, *Frederick the Second*; Joseph MacCabe and Henri Lammens *ut supra*.

[2] See Note G, p. 75.

[3] See Note H, p. 75.

the most dangerous enemy of the mediæval Papacy was the Emperor Frederick II of the house of Hohenstaufen, the son of Henry VI by a Norman princess, through whom he inherited the Sicilian crown. A southerner rather than a German by training and temperament, a pronounced free-thinker and an expert in the new developments in physical science, which the Arabs had introduced into Europe, besides being an autocratic ruler of a " totalitarian " type, Frederick found himself opposed to the Papacy in his dual capacity of Italian despot (his hold over Germany was always precarious and he took little interest in his Teutonic dominions), and of free-thinking savant.

His effort to unite the political anti-Papal rôle of the Holy Roman Empire with the anti-Catholic rôle of the new secular civilization, is one of the most fascinating chapters in the history of the Middle Ages, and was, probably, the most formidable opposition that the Papacy had to encounter throughout that entire epoch. The memory of the mediæval " Antichrist " is enshrined in that Catholic *Who's Who* of the nether world, the *Inferno* of Dante, and the fear that his audacious attempt excited is infallibly demonstrated by the ferocious war of extermination that was waged after his death by the Church against the remains of the " viper's brood ", the Imperial dynasty of the Hohenstaufen.

Frederick Hohenstaufen was the greatest monarch of the Middle Ages, and, indeed, in the variety and brilliance of his mental endowments ranks probably among the half-dozen most gifted individuals who have occupied a throne. But for the Catholic terror which posthumously destroyed his work and dynasty, he would undoubtedly be recognized as the initiator of the uninterrupted renaissance of European civilization : the first and by far the greatest monarch of the Renaissance.

Side by side with the burgeoning of the Italian Renaissance there burst into brilliant bloom a secular Provençal culture, in which a highly developed literature of carnal love existed in curious juxtaposition to the gloomy and rapidly spreading Manichean doctrine, which taught the criminality of all fleshly attachments, and advocated a Buddhistic doctrine of racial extinction as a remedy for the perennial and incurable ills of mankind. By the beginning of the thirteenth century Provence was virtually lost to Christianity, and while none of its principalities and city republics possessed the political power to challenge the Papacy, yet both the great wealth of this rich province and its central position in the heart of Catholic Europe, made its loss an extremely serious matter for the Roman See.

The Oriental civilization had, in fact, driven a wedge into the heart of Christian Europe. The problem for Papal Christianity was, either to split this wedge by force, or be forcibly split by it. Such in brief was the situation which the crisis of the thirteenth century presented to the Papacy.

The place occupied in the story of human kind by the history of theocracy, and of sacerdotal civilization in general, is a peculiar one. A theocratic civilization, like those of ancient Egypt and of mediæval Europe, may be defined briefly as a civilization at tether ; that is, it is a civilization which is held close to the temple, and cannot stray far from its central shrine, or from the revelation in whose honour that shrine is erected. Consequently, a clerical civilization is a fixed civilization, metaphysical in its thought, and traditional in its world outlook. Such a culture can be only scholastic in character, since, through its whole duration and underlying all its manifestations, its interest in the present is bounded by, and subordinated to, its respect for the past.

It is, in fact, a universal law of every theocracy, from ancient Babylon to modern Tibet, and of every society guided by ecclesiastical authority, that, as a modern theologian has aptly remarked : " There are no problems to solve, there are only authorities to consult." Such a system of life and thought cannot admit real change, genuine evolution, or the need for finding new answers to old questions, since the answer, the final and definitive answer, to the old riddles that confront humanity was given by revelation in the distant past. It is, in fact, a necessary postulate of any theocratic culture based on divine revelation that there has been some bygone age in human history wherein man was not merely wiser, but—thanks to revelation—finally and unalterably wiser than he can ever be again.

Hence at the centre of every sacerdotal culture the intellectual enquirer will find the notice : " No thoroughfare " ; and this warning to human thought is generally accompanied by another : " Trespassers will be "—not " prosecuted ", but rather " exterminated ".

For just as it was sacrilege, punishable by certain

death, to enter the physical Holy of Holies of the Temple, so is it equally sacrilege to enter the Holy of Holies of the revelation upon whose unseen foundation the temple is built. In such a social state it is blasphemy to " gang o'er the fundamentals ", which must be preserved static and inviolable to prying thoughts ; and in a society wherein change is the effective sin against the Holy Ghost, the first law of human thought is to negate itself and to deny the curiosity which is the driving motive of the human mind in action.

Accordingly, in every theocracy, in every " totalitarian " régime, like that of the mediæval Papacy, curiosity, the desire to know which constitutes the vitality of thought, is the first and essential crime, and in some form or other the law against " dangerous thoughts " is fundamental in such an Authoritarian system.

These psychological principles led, logically and directly, in the thirteenth century to the inauguration of the Catholic Terror ; the most ruthless and sustained repression of human volition and human thought that mankind has ever known in the entire course of its historic evolution.

The Papacy escaped from the earlier perils represented by the barbarians, by the agency of violence ; first, of the Franks against its local enemies, then of the Crusaders against the world of Islam. The menace of the thirteenth century was of another, a civilized order, and as such required the suppression of ideas. Civilization involves ideas, and it is an old legend that ideas cannot be killed by physical violence. The thirteenth-century Papacy set itself the task of disproving this legend. That it succeeded in so doing, to a very large extent at least, is demonstrated by the undeniable fact of its survival down to the present day, a survival which must be held to prove the practicability of suppressing progressive ideas over a long period and of artificially checking the natural course of civilization and of evolutionary forces.

But for the Catholic terror, inaugurated—in so far as a complex development can be attributed to any one man—by Pope Innocent III (1198-1216), when he began the Crusade against heresy and by his immediate successors who founded the mediæval Inquisition, there can be little doubt that Catholicism would have begun to disintegrate at this time, or that European civilization would now be much more advanced, and would have solved many of the problems and shed many of the superstitions which still confront it to-day.

Whereas in the eleventh century the Papacy had directed the Crusade against the infidel, in the thirteenth it directed the same battering-ram against the heretic, who is, in ecclesiastical eyes, so often worse than the infidel. In order to crush the higher civilization of Sicily and Provence, the inhabitants of the more backward areas of Europe were called in, in particular France, who earned her subsequent title of " eldest daughter of the church " by the prominent part which Simon de Montfort, Charles of Anjou, and other barons took in the bloody suppression of the heretics and the secular culture of Provence in the Crusade against the Albigenses at the beginning of the

century, and fifty years later against the Hohenstaufen dynasty in Naples and Sicily. The battle
of Muret (1213) terminated the war against the
Provençal heretics ; the battles of Benevento (1265)
and Tagliacozzo (1268) overthrew the power of
the Hohenstaufen dynasty in Italy, removing
successively Manfred, the illegitimate son of the
great Frederick, and Conradin his legitimate grand-
son, with whom perished the house of Hohenstaufen, so long the bugbear of the Papal power.
The Papacy escaped the first shock of the crisis by
resort to the sword.

To kill a heretic is always easier than to argue
with him ; the more formidable his arguments,
the more is this true. But, since thought is a
recurrent phenomenon of civilization, when once
it has passed a certain stage, the passing violence
of military expeditions is not sufficient to cope
with it permanently. Europe had now reached
this stage in human development, and its natural
evolution towards a scientific and secular world
outlook was too strong to be permanently checked.
Heresy became an endemic crop, ranging from the
most advanced philosophical criticism to the most
fantastic superstition ; but all were alike, however, in their hostility to the Papacy.

To check this deeply-rooted tendency, it
was necessary to organize repression on a permanent, ubiquitous, and scientific basis. Heresy
must be systematically watched, systematically
fought, systematically exterminated. It was for
these purposes that the Popes created the Inquisition, the most terrible engine of repression
that the world has ever known, which down to the

seventeenth century—and in Spain down to the end of the eighteenth—burnt amid whole forests of stakes the living bodies of innumerable heretics. By the very fact of its establishment, the thirteenth-century Papacy took up the position of gaoler of mankind whose forward movement must at all costs be checked. This fact alone is sufficient to demonstrate that that century marks the point at which the Papacy ceased to have a progressive rôle in European society.

The Catholic terror inaugurated by the Inquisition was something new in human experience ; essentially it represented the reduction of terrorism to a set of scientific principles. If heresy was not to prevail, the heretic must be exterminated as fast as he appeared. To the mediæval inquisitor, as to the modern political police of the " totalitarian " state, the axiom " truth must prevail " appeared a self-evident falsehood, for how could truth express itself except through the mouths of men, and how could men express it in an effective manner from the solitude of the Holy Office dungeon or amid the crackle of the destroying flames ?

The inquisition realized, as its modern successors, the Gestapo and the Cheka, have also realized, that it is quite possible to destroy dissident opinion and that the blood of the martyrs need not necessarily be the seed of the church, always provided that persecution has a permanent and not a spasmodic character, and that its technique can be developed to a point at which " heretic " and " martyr " become exact equivalents.

This new and terribly efficacious " science " of terrorism, by means of which the Papacy saved itself from destruction in the crisis of the thirteenth century, was admirably summarized in a single pregnant and immortal sentence by the answer of the Papal legate in the Albigensian Crusade to an over-scrupulous Crusader who desired to differentiate between the Catholic and heretical population in a captured town. " Kill them all, my son ; at the day of judgement God will know how to distinguish."

Here, in a sentence, we find summed up the " science " by whose means the Papacy preserved itself in the thirteenth century, the " science " of permanent terrorism, and it is evident to the well-informed critic that this " science " must have reached a very high degree of perfection to achieve its purpose so long and to hold the awakening reason of Europe in chains throughout an entire epoch.

In fact, just as it is evident that the author of *Hamlet* was acquainted, at least empirically, with the " inferiority complex " and divided personality of modern psychology, of which phenomena the play gives the classical demonstration, it is likewise apparent that all those doctrines of organized terrorism which the scientific ingenuity of twentieth-century technique places at the disposal of modern dictators for the purpose of extinguishing the lamp of human reason were already well known, in fact if not in theory, to the mediæval terrorists of the Inquisition. It is evident furthermore that they saved the Catholic doctrine from the onslaughts of human reason, and the Papal power from the corroding scepticism of the human intellect, by suppression as drastically ruthless, and by terrorism as technically complete, as if the familiars of the Holy Office had read Trotsky and observed Hitler, before applying with deadly efficiency the theory and practice of these modern masters.[1]

It was above all by means of the " science " of terrorism that the Papacy was enabled to save itself from the genuine science of the thirteenth century, and it was above all by the agency of the Catholic terror that the Papacy, from the thirteenth century onwards, was enabled to survive in a world that became ever more indifferent to its claims and sceptical as to its divine origin.

Note F : Acts of Vandalism

Both the original Arab Crusaders of Islam and the later Christian Crusaders were semi-barbarians, and acted as such. The burning of the Alexandrian library by the Arabs—or rather the burning of what was left of it after previous Christian con-flagrations—finds an exact parallel in the destruction of the library of the Emir of Edessa by the later Christian Crusaders. On the whole, of the two barbarian armies the Arabs probably come out the better ; their ravages were, to some extent at least, checked by the humanitarian precepts of the Koran, and the capture of Jerusalem by the Khalif Omar, where the inhabitants were admitted to quarter (A.D. 636), was certainly a much milder affair than the wholesale massacre of seventy thousand unarmed inhabitants, and the burning alive of the Jews, in 1099, on the recapture of

[1] See Note J, p. 76.

Jerusalem by the crusading army of Godfrey de Bouillon.

Note G

" In short, the Troubadour movement and the Age of Chivalry were inspired from the Moslem world, through Languedoc and Barcelona, through south Italy, and in part through the Crusades." Joseph MacCabe, *The Splendour of Moorish Spain*, p. 238.

Note H : *Manicheanism*

Manicheanism, a variation of Persian Zoroastrianism, was first expounded by Mani, a Babylonian teacher, in the third century A.D. Later it was widely diffused throughout both Europe and Western Asia. St Augustine was a Manichean at one stage of his career; his greatest work, the *City of God*, is derived from Manichean sources, and its central conception of the " two cities " —good and evil—is Manichean rather than Christian in character. The Manicheans, under various names, were consistently persecuted both by Christian and Mohammedan rulers; this was due probably to their asceticism rather than to their dualistic philosophy, and the Catholic hostility to birth-control probably dates from the repudiation of their doctrine entirely forbidding carnal intercourse. So ruthless was the persecution directed against them that we know very little about the European sects which adhered to their doctrines.

In Provence they seem to have been completely exterminated. They were sometimes known as " Cathari "—" the perfect ones "—from the title adopted by their clergy, and also as " Albigenses," from a fortuitous connection established between their sect and the town of Albi in Provence.

Note J

The thoroughness of the terror set up by the Inquisition is effectively demonstrated by the complete destruction of the two most famous heretical works of the later Middle Ages : the *De Tribus Impostoribus*, ascribed to the Emperor Frederick Hohenstaufen without contradiction in his lifetime, and the *Everlasting Gospel*, published about 1260, and ascribed to the mediæval mystic, Joachim of Flora, the Gospel of the " Spiritual Franciscans " who were exterminated by the Inquisition on account of their attacks on the luxury of the Church and the Papal court. So completely have these once famous works disappeared, that doubts have even been raised as to their having ever existed. We know, in fact, as little of the mediæval enemies of the Church as—to initiate a parallel to which we shall recur—of the enemies of Fascism in present-day Germany, or of those of Bolshevism in contemporary Russia. Trotsky, the supreme theorist of modern terrorism, himself remarks in his classical work on the subject : " Let us first regard the religious reformation, which proved the watershed between the Middle Ages and modern history. The deeper were the interests of the masses that it involved, the wider was its sweep, the more fiercely did the civil war develop under the religious banner, and the more merciless did the terror become on the other side." [1]

[1] Leon Trotsky, *The Defence of Terrorism*, p. 46 of 2nd English Edition.

CHAPTER IV

FOURTH CRISIS

THE PROTESTANT REFORMATION

(a) *THE CRISIS*

THE causes of the Protestant Reformation are so well known that it is unnecessary to devote much space to enumerating them, particularly as the theological controversies which arose at that period, are even yet not quite extinct. It will, accordingly, be sufficient to glance briefly at the crisis itself, before passing on to the remedy adopted by the Papacy, a remedy whose nature has been but little understood by the historians of the intervening period. These causes fall under two distinct and separate headings : (*a*) The intellectual revolution which characterized the era ; (*b*) The exploitation of the Teutonic countries by the Papacy. It is necessary to glance at each of these causes in turn.

With regard to the first cause, the intellectual revolution of the sixteenth century is thus eloquently summarized by a modern historian.

" For, indeed, a change was coming upon the world the meaning and direction of which even still is hidden from us, a change from era to era. The paths trodden by the history of ages were broken up, old things were passing away, and the faith and life of ten centuries were dissolving like a dream. Chivalry was dying, the abbey and the castle were soon together to crumble into ruins, and all the forms, desires, beliefs, convictions of the old world were passing away, never to return. A new continent had risen up beyond the Western sea. The floor of heaven, inlaid with stars, had sunk back into an infinite abyss of immeasurable space, and the firm earth itself, unfixed from its foundations, was seen to be but a small atom in the vastness of the universe. In the fabric of habit in which they had so laboriously built for themselves, mankind were to remain no longer." [1]

Simultaneously the introduction of printing opened the way for popular education ; geographical discovery revolutionized the conception of the earth, and astronomical discovery that of the heavens. The parochial universe disappeared into insignificance.

The effect of all this upon the Roman Catholic church is easily understandable. It came to Europe as a shock that, for the previous twelve centuries, the intellect of Western civilization had been monopolized and controlled by an " infallible " church, which had yet taught an astronomy, a geography and an anatomy which were now all proved to be false or defective. If the Church could make so many mistakes with regard to the map of the Earth, what guarantee was there that its map of heaven was any more correct ? The geographical

[1] J. A. Froude, *History of England*, Vol. I, ch. i.

discoveries of Columbus, Da Gama and Magellan, the scientific discoveries of Vesalius, Copernicus and Galileo, popularized and made universal by the printing-presses of Caxton and his confrères, undermined the authority of the Church at every point, by proving what the technically less-equipped Arab savants had only guessed, that the earth was round and the heavens infinite.

In a world where revolutions in knowledge were the order of the day, what tradition could remain sacrosanct and inviolable? Why should the authority of Aquinas survive that of his master Aristotle? Why should the world of revelation alone remain immune from the sphere of change? In such a world of permanent revolution, the Papacy, with its motto *Semper eadem*, "For ever the same," stood in immediate, particular and deadly danger.

The intellectual revolution, however, while indirectly assisting the Protestant Reformation by weakening the forces that were favourable to established tradition, was not the immediate cause of the great religious upheaval of the sixteenth century. That this was so can be seen from the dogmatic and generally anti-intellectual attitude of the bulk of the reformers themselves, who stood in the sharpest opposition both to the literary humanism of the Renaissance and to the advance of contemporary science.

With regard to humanism, it was by no means an accident that the great humanists of the epoch, Erasmus, Thomas More and Rabelais, adhered to the Roman Church and opposed the Reformation. With regard to science it is well known how

Luther denounced " the whore reason " and jeered at the heliocentric theory of the earth's motion, while Calvin burnt Servetus, and the Scotch Calvinists surpassed all others in their gloomy bigotry and in the ferocious thoroughness with which they carried out the biblical injunction " Thou shalt not suffer a witch to live." It is evident from such examples, which could be multiplied indefinitely, that the Protestant Reformation was in fact very far from being, as in Protestant legend, the triumph of light over darkness.

That this was so, was due to the second, the immediate and decisive, cause of the Reformation ; the ruthless exploitation of northern Europe by the Italian Papacy. This extortion, which had already caused the Hussite (Bohemian) wars of the fifteenth century, had by the opening of the sixteenth assumed monstrous proportions, when the north, and Germany in particular, whose political weakness, consequent upon its divisions, favoured and facilitated papal exploitation, was systematically bled white by a multiplicity of ecclesiastical taxes of one kind or another. It was not by any means an accident that the original protest of Luther, which was the starting-point of the Reformation, was caused by the promulgation of a Papal indulgence, the object of which was the collection of money for the building of St Peter's Cathedral at Rome, nor was it in any way an accident that the whole German nation forthwith rallied behind its bold spokesman.

In brief, the Reformation was in its essence not a struggle between light and darkness, still less between Protestant enlightenment and Catholic ignorance, but one between exploiters and exploited ; in a word, it was a revolt of the most exploited, and therefore most backward, parts and peoples of Europe. It was again far from being an accident that the lands where the Reformation acquired the greatest power, Scotland and Sweden, were two of the most backward and isolated countries in Europe.

In his work previously quoted, Karl Kautsky thus summarizes the economic and cultural character of the Reformation :

" That Italy, France, and Spain remained Catholic is not to be ascribed to their spiritual backwardness, but rather to their higher economic development. They were the masters of the Pope ; through him they exploited Teutonic Christendom, which was compelled to separate from the Papacy in order to escape exploitation, but at the cost of severing its ties with the wealthiest and most highly developed countries in Europe. In so far the Reformation was a struggle of Barbarism against Civilization. . . . This is, of course, not to be understood as a condemnation of the Reformation. We have recorded the above facts because they explain why the most cultivated minds in Germany, as in England, would have nothing to do with the Reformation, which is unintelligible if we adopt the traditional view that the Reformation was essentially of a spiritual nature, a struggle between Protestant light and Catholic darkness.

" On the contrary, Humanism was in complete antagonism to the Reformation." [1]

[1] Kautsky, *op. cit.*, pp. 59-60.

The above facts indicate the character of the Reformation and explain its nature. In those countries where the backwardness and poverty of the people made any transfer of wealth elsewhere a heavy burden, i.e. in such lands as Germany, Scotland, Scandinavia and later the Netherlands —ruthlessly exploited by the Pope's ally and protector, the King of Spain—the Reformation became a mass movement, whereas in Southern Europe it did not extend far beyond a narrow circle of intellectuals. England and France occupied an intermediate position. In England, the royal power supported a moderate version of the Reformation, which was thus enabled to prevail, whereas in France the Protestants or Huguenots allied themselves with the still undeveloped bourgeoisie, and consequently failed to obtain control of the State power.

This fundamental character of the Reformation stood revealed in the map of Europe in the middle of the sixteenth century, when a line drawn across the centre of the continent marked the boundary between the shrunken dominions of the Roman Church and the territories occupied by its Lutheran and Calvinist rivals. As a result of this transformation the Roman Catholic Church had ceased to be *the* church, and had become merely one among several churches. Could it survive such an anomalous position, one so far removed from its mediæval claims and from its continued assumption of a ubiquitous prerogative ?

At first sight it would appear not, particularly as both the spirit of the age and the course of economic and intellectual development now began to move strongly and continuously from the countries of the Mediterranean seaboard, which still remained faithful to the Papacy, to those of the Atlantic seaboard, such as England and Holland, which either had adhered, or were about to adhere, to the reformed churches. In the course which historic evolution was setting, and in the larger air of the modern world, it seemed that the Papacy was doomed to perish. But once again it escaped from the shadow of death, this time by the agency of the most original and extraordinary of all its manifestations of vitality and adaptability.

(b) THE SOLUTION

The Papacy had succeeded in escaping from the preceding crisis by adopting and adapting to its service the Mohammedan institution of the Holy War or Crusade. In the sixteenth century it likewise effected its deliverance from the Protestant crisis by adopting and utilizing another Mohammedan institution, the order of Dervishes, regimented by an iron discipline and organized on military lines for the salvation of the Church and the world expansion of the Roman See ; for such, there is little room to doubt, was the origin and derivation of the celebrated " Company of Jesus ", founded in 1536 by Ignatius Loyola for the express purpose of converting the Mohammedan world, but by circumstances, and in particular by the favour accorded to it by the Papacy, eventually transformed into the great propagandist and missionary Order of the Church, primarily against the Protestant heresies of the Reformers.

Even when the fullest allowance has been made for the operation of all those social and economic causes usually embraced within the scope of " historical materialism ", it seems beyond question that but for Ignatius Loyola and his Company of Jesus the Roman church would have perished, or at least been reduced to insignificance, in the storms of the Reformation era. Jesuitism was the method which it evolved for its salvation ; and the Catholic Counter-Reformation cannot be separated from the name and fame of Ignatius Loyola and his disciples. But for their opportune appearance it is most unlikely that the Papacy single-handed could have stemmed the flood.

In fact, the history of the Catholic Church, throughout the epoch between the Protestant Reformation and the French Revolution, without the Jesuits, would resemble a modern history of Socialism which entirely omitted from consideration the school of Karl Marx.

The story of Ignatius Loyola is too well known to need retelling, the unceasing propaganda of the Jesuits, for so long the educational instructors of Catholic Europe, has ensured that the romantic story of its founder, the Spanish knight wounded in the war against France, who devotes himself on his bed of sickness to the Papacy which had inherited the keys of Heaven, should go the round of the world.

While the Jesuits have taken care to popularize the memory of their Founder, the actual origins of the famous Society remained unknown down to the end of the nineteenth century, when Hermann Müller first demonstrated the close affinity between the Jesuit Congregation and its peculiar constitution, and the Mohammedan orders of Dervishes long domiciled in Moorish Spain.[1]

As Müller has shown, it was by no means an accident that Loyola originally set out to convert the Mohammedan world, or that his secretary and intimate adviser was Polanco, a Jew not converted to Christianity until middle age. It should be remembered that the Jews worked on most harmonious terms with the Mohammedans, and were, in fact, often the principal missionaries of the Arab-Moorish culture.[2]

Müller has subjected the doctrines peculiar to Jesuitism to a detailed examination, and has compared them both with the peculiar doctrines of the earlier Catholic orders, and with those of the Dervish orders of the world of Islam. His conclusion, at the end of this examination, is that what was essential to Jesuitism, and gave it its peculiar character and strength, was derived from Islam and not from the Mediæval Catholic Church.[3]

The three fundamental characteristics which distinguished the Jesuit order were : (a) The despotic power conceded to Loyola and his successors as Generals of the Order ; (b) The " corpse-like " obedience—*perinde cadaver*—which the individual Jesuit vowed in the service of his order and its head ;[4] (c) The distinctively military character which has always marked the order,

---

[1] Hermann Müller, *Les Origines de la Compagnie de Jésus—Ignace et Lainez*, 1898.

[2] *Cf.* Joseph McCabe, *The Splendour of Moorish Spain.*

[3] See Note K., p. 94.

[4] *Cf.* Loyola's *Letter on Obedience* to the Portuguese Jesuits, 1553.

and which is expressly indicated in its original Spanish title. Müller has shown that there is no real counterpart to these features in the earlier Catholic orders, but that all of them bear the closest resemblance, even verbally, to the earlier constitutions of the Mohammedan Dervish orders. The same also applies to the famous motto of the company, *Ad majorem Dei gloriam*.[1]

The Jesuit " Company " was, in fact, an organization of storm-troops designed for a specific end : the defeat of the enemies of the Church. It represented, indeed, the exact adaptation needed to meet the aggressive revolution that was threatening to submerge Papacy and Church alike in a common ruin. The Papacy, in accepting the novel forms of service which the redoubtable Fathers offered it, in recognizing the " Company " and in bestowing upon it the freedom from monastic routine necessary for its peculiar work, was guided by that adaptation to circumstances which has so pre-eminently distinguished the Papacy throughout its many vicissitudes. But it must not be supposed that the Papacy ever readily parted with powers so extraordinary, or that, in its heart, it loved its too powerful auxiliary whose influence threatened several times to swallow up its own.

The Jesuits have, in fact, always been the Frankenstein monster of the Papacy, but a monster necessary to fight off the even worse monsters outside the Church. Jesuitism has always been an independent power, making its own terms with

---

[1] *Cf.* Neuman and Baretti, *Spanish Dictionary*, s.v. " Compania " —Company, troop, a body of soldiers under the command of a captain "—*i.e.* an essentially military formation.

the Roman See, rather than the humble auxiliary of its professed vows.[1]

A Protestant historian thus describes the real relations which existed between the Papacy and the ecclesiastical " Prætorian Guard " which had interposed itself between the Papal throne and the heretical powers which would destroy it.

" Without the Jesuits the Papacy would certainly not have become once more a great power in the eyes of the nations, and yet Sixtus V (1585-90) was inspired by the right feeling, when he found himself unable to conquer his dislike of the order. If we reflect upon the idea of the Papacy, and upon the great men who embody it, we feel loath to leave this Pope. He is the last for centuries who is really interesting. Not the least reason for this is that the Jesuits succeeded in guiding the destinies of the church. The Black Pope gradually takes his place beside the white one, or, to use another metaphor, the Pope becomes more and more like the king in a game of chess. It is of course the soldiers' first duty to protect the king, but the king has a very limited power of moving, and he is only allowed to take part in the battle so long as he does not endanger the victory. The Pope remains the representative of Christ to whom the Jesuits have sworn to be faithful even unto death, but their general is the leader, and the " Company of Jesus " is the guard. Will it be possible to avoid friction with such an

[1] See Note L, p. 95.

arrangement, and will military subordination stand the test ? " [1]

To draw an apposite parallel, which will be used again in the latter part of this book, the Jesuits were the Fascists of the sixteenth century. They saved the Papal church by a mixture of demagogy and terrorism, of mediæval atavism and of adaptability to modern conditions, but they saved it only on their own terms, terms which the Papacy did not relish, but which it was forced, none the less, to accept, as the sole alternative to destruction.

Just as the Fascist militia, following the " leader " in blind obedience, first saves the ruling class of to-day, and then binds upon it burdens grievous and onerous, which, none the less, dire necessity compels it to accept in order to stem the rising tide of economic democracy, so in the revolutionary era of the sixteenth century the Jesuits, the " Papal Militia ", exacted similarly onerous terms as the price of their equally indispensable assistance, when led by their " general " (*Dux—Duce*) against the rising tide of contemporary religious democracy ; the resemblance, indeed, extended even to their methods.

The Papacy, however, can no more dispense with the Jesuits than the present-day political reaction can with the Fascists. As long as the Reformation remained aggressive, the Jesuits remained necessary. It was not until 1773, when " enthusiasm " was at a discount in Protestant

[1] Gustav Krüger, *The Papacy*, pp. 197-198.

countries, that the Papacy plucked up courage to dissolve the famous Company, with the enthusiastic concurrence of the contemporary Catholic world. Only a generation later—1773-1814—the storms of the revolutionary era, inaugurated by the Jacobins, compelled Pope Pius VII to undo the work of his predecessor, Clement XIV, and restore the *corps d'élite* of the Catholic Church to meet the storms of a new era of crisis.[1]

It is well known how the Jesuit Counter-Reformation met, checked, and partially drove back the tide of Protestant revolution, during the memorable century of the religious conflict which endured from 1536, that epochal year which witnessed the actual foundation of the Jesuit movement, the death of Erasmus, the last mediator between Catholic and Protestant theology, and the publication of Calvin's *Institutes*—the *Das Kapital* of the Reformation—and the year 1648, which saw the end of the " Thirty Years' War " and the division of Europe on religious lines that have endured, substantially unaltered, down to the present day.

It is well known also how the Jesuits effected this result, astounding in view of the manifold forces which the spirit of the age arrayed against them, by a combination of the most divergent methods, force and guile being equally conspicuous in their plan of campaign, and how every weapon in the arsenals of contemporary society was utilized by them, from the development of a new pedagogic system to a " scientific " doctrine of regicide, in which they demonstrated their

[1] See Note M, p. 96.

capacity to equal the famous Mohammedan sect whose collateral relations they actually were.[1]

Karl Kautsky thus summarizes the historic rôle and achievements of Jesuitism :

" Jesuitism is Humanism at a lower mental level, robbed of its spiritual independence, rigidly organized and pressed in the service of the church. Jesuitism resembles Humanism as the Christianity of the Imperial Age resembled Neoplatonism. It is the form in which the Catholic Church embraced Humanism and brought herself up to date, abandoning the feudal outlook for the outlook which dominated society from the sixteenth to the eighteenth centuries. Jesuitism became the most formidable power of the reformed Catholic Church because it was more in harmony with the new economic and political conditions. It wrought its effects by virtue of the same forces that Humanism had made use of, by the superiority of classical education, by influencing princes, and paying heed to the financial powers. Like the Humanists, the Jesuits fostered absolute power, but only in the cases of princes for whom they laboured. Like the Humanists, they did not think it incompatible with their monarchical sentiments to remove princes who did not suit their purpose." [2]

The Papacy backed up the Jesuits, not merely by the direct support which it gave them, but by the extensive reforms in manners and morals—not forgetting itself—which accompanied the Catholic Counter-Reformation which it conducted. Gone

[1] See Note N, p. 97.   [2] Kautsky, *op. cit.*, p. 71.

were the licentious days of the Borgias and of the artistic trifling and thinly disguised scepticism which had marked the times of the Medici Popes. Just as the Papacy ceased to produce artists it began to bring forth saints. Michelangelo (1475-1564), the most religious artist of the Renaissance, who survived Ignatius Loyola, forms, so to speak, a bridge between the two epochs.

Even in the sphere of doctrine, though intransigence greeted the efforts of moderate men like Melanchthon on the Protestant side, and Cardinal Pole on the Catholic, to bridge the gulf between the two religious worlds, yet the Council of Trent at least defined' the Catholic position clearly, and ended such abuses as the sale of indulgences which had started the Reformation. The net result of the Counter-Reformation was the transformation of the mediæval Catholic Church into the Catholicism of modern times, the distinctively " Roman ", centralized Catholicism, of which St Ignatius is as definitely the founder as was Hildebrand (St Gregory VII) of mediæval Catholicism, or St Benedict of the Catholicism of the Dark Ages, or as St Peter is alleged to have been of that of ancient times. The modern epoch in Roman Catholic Church history has been essentially the epoch of the Jesuits.

A Protestant historian of the era of the Reformation thus sums up the net effect of the Catholic Counter-Reformation which the Jesuits conducted and the Council of Trent officially endorsed :

" The Church was thus both reformed and narrowed by the decrees of the Council of Trent.

Henceforth it tolerated within its fold neither the old diversity of doctrine on the one hand, nor the old laxity of morals on the other hand, and henceforth it was by no means coextensive with Western Christendom, as it had once been. It is now generally called the ' Roman Catholic Church ', to distinguish it from the ' Catholic Church ' of the Middle Ages, from which it, and so many other churches, have sprung." [1]

Thus the Papacy emerged from the terrible crisis of the sixteenth century which ushered in modern history. But it escaped at a heavy price, for while it checked the Protestant advance, it could not altogether extirpate the new heresies either in the old world or the new. As a result, in place of the division of the Christian world into the fundamental sections of East and West, Greek and Latin, a third, Protestant section had to be admitted, as a permanent addition to the religious map.

None the less, the Papacy may be said to have enjoyed a substantial triumph, since it not merely survived, but survived as still by far the strongest and most homogeneous of all the Christian ecclesiastical authorities ; and with an authority inside and over its own Church extending rapidly to the proportions of a permanent dictatorship, as a result of, and an answer to, the external danger which now threatened, also permanently, the pre-eminence, the authority, even the very existence of the Roman Catholic Church.

[1] Frederick Seebohm, *The Era of the Protestant Revolution*, p. 208. The Council of Trent sat, with intervals, from 1545 to 1564.

Note K: The Dervish Orders

From at least the eleventh century onwards, regular orders of dervishes appeared in the world of Islam. Morocco, which remained on the closest terms with Moorish Spain, was one of the chief centres of their influence. The Dervishes were vowed to blind obedience to the head of their order, who was endowed with despotic power. Long before Hermann Müller pointed out the extraordinary similarity even in words, between their constitutions and those of the Jesuits, acute Protestant critics had already detected a strong Mohammedan influence in the *Spiritual Exercises* of Loyola, whose imagery in particular, has the stark, unshaded character peculiar to the Koran.[1] Polanco, the converted Jew who became the secretary of Ignatius, and whom Papal opposition alone prevented from being elected fourth General of the Order in 1572, was one of the two men besides the founder whose actual influence on the Company must be taken into account. Polanco and Lainez, Loyola's immediate successor as General of the Company (1558-1565), played in the annals of Jesuitism the part of Talleyrand and Fouché to the Napoleonic rôle of the founder himself.

[1] Isaac Taylor, *Ignatius Loyola and the Rudiments of Jesuitism* (1849), p. 208.

Note L

The Protestant theologian, Isaac Taylor, acutely remarks in relation to the independent status of the Jesuit organization :

"It is easy to fall into the error of supposing that Jesuitism, which at the first so signally came to the aid of the Roman church in its time of need, and which has made so many professions of devotedness to its service, is itself a mere appendage of that church ; or that it is a sort of emphatic Romanism or that it stands on level ground along with the other religious orders, and that it is related to the Papacy nearly as they are. Such an idea of the Society as this is not merely contradicted by every page of its history, but is incompatible with its spirit and its rudiments. Jesuitism may outlast Romanism ; or it may be wholly severed from it, and yet, may live and grow. Often, as the Society has been seen prostrate at the feet of the supreme pontiff venting itself in vehement protestations of loyalty, it has, in fact, always hung loose upon ecclesiastical Catholicism, and has shown itself to be organically independent, living by its own root and fibres. Jesuitism has its own purposes to secure, and its own law of self-preservation." (Isaac Taylor, *Ignatius Loyola and the Rudiments of Jesuitism.*)

Note M : *Jesuitism and Fascism*

In recent years it has been the fashion to compare Loyola with Lenin, and Jesuitism with Bolshevism. It is, however, obvious that the comparison is misleading, at any rate if it is intended in any sense that transcends a merely personal comparison of qualities. Essentially, Jesuitism was a retrograde, a counter-revolutionary movement, and if one seeks an analogous influence in the political world of the twentieth century, it is to Fascism, not to Communism, that one must look. Actually, the sixteenth-century analogy to Bolshevism was Calvinism, which was similarly revolutionary and iconoclastic towards tradition. In this connection the author has written elsewhere :

" In this sense we may compare the movement of twentieth-century Fascism with the Jesuit movement of the sixteenth century, a movement which, in the era of the Catholic Counter-Reformation, similarly strove to check the tide of progress and to preserve the Roman Church from a decay which was visibly threatening to engulf it. Indeed, this historic parallel extends further, to the social character and the methods of the two movements. . . . Just as Cardinal Bellarmine, Father Suarez, and their coadjutors, represented in the seventeenth century the high-water-mark of propaganda as it was then understood, so the propagandists of Fascism have likewise mastered the technique of their craft. . . .

" . . . It will then be seen that the particular

features of the Fascist order are exactly combined to combat anti-capitalist revolution in the present age, just as it is easy to observe in retrospect that the Jesuit Counter-Reformation in the sixteenth century was also exactly designed to meet not the general menace of " heresy ", but the particular heresies of Protestantism which threatened the traditional social-ecclesiastical order of mediæval Christianity in the age of the Reformation."—Ridley, *At the Cross Roads of History*, p. 97.

Note N : *The Jesuits and Regicide*

Several Jesuit writers defended regicide, particularly Mariana, the Spanish historian. Several Protestant or lukewarm rulers were murdered, apparently at the instigation of the Jesuits, or by their pupils, the most famous being Henry III and Henry IV of France (1589-1610) and William the Silent of Orange (1584). The Jesuits seem to have been privy to Babington's plot to murder Elizabeth, and to the Gunpowder plot of 1605, for participation in which their English provincial, Garnet, suffered death, apparently on convincing evidence. Jesuit books advocating regicide were burnt by the hangman in both England and France.

The " Assassins " were a heretical Mohammedan sect founded by Hasan ben Sabah in the eleventh century. They were destroyed by the Tartars. They trained a class of professional murderers, the Dais or disciples, who " removed " obnoxious rulers. These murderers, before setting out, were drugged with hashish, hence their name " Hashishin ", corrupted into " Assassins ". It is very

G

unlikely that Loyola had any direct knowledge of this order, which was execrated by the Muslim world on account of its heresies, and had, in any case, vanished from the scene long before the advent of the Jesuits. (Cf. De Lacy O'Leary, *A Short history of the Fatimid Khalifat*, and Prof. E. G. Browne, *Literary History of Persia*, Vol. II.) Mme. B. Bouthoul, in *Le Grand Maitre des Assassins* (*i.e.* Hasan Ben Sabah), p. 227, says : " Among the Jesuits we shall find this autocratic organization, the flair for action, the habit of not recognizing any authority except their own. A body of men uniquely devoted to their work, living a life half monastic, half military, capable when necessary of mingling in the life of their age without losing their moral integrity, while remaining, following a rule derived from the Mussulman orders, under the jurisdiction of their head. Whence the supreme importance of the general among them as among their models. We know the hatreds, the mystification, and the legends relating to the Jesuits, as formerly to the Templars and the Assassins."

In 1614 a pamphlet appeared in Paris, bearing the title : *Assassination of the King or Maxims of the Old Man of the Vatican Mountain and his Assassins practised at the expense of the person of the late King Henry the Great.*

The Assassins referred to were the Jesuits, whose pupil, Ravaillac, murdered Henry on May 14, 1610.

CHAPTER V

FIFTH CRISIS

THE LIBERAL REVOLUTION

(a) *THE CRISIS*

THE course of human history hitherto has revealed the alternate domination of contrary types of civilization. In succession, the panorama reveals the evolution of the theocratic and sacerdotal civilizations of the ancient East, the secular and predominantly rationalistic culture of antiquity, the reversion to a sacerdotal theocracy in the Catholic Middle Ages, and the revival of a secular and rationalist culture in modern times. In this cultural lineage it is obvious that each of these four great civilizations was far more like its penultimate than its immediate predecessor. Thus we can compare " ancient " civilization with " modern ", but hardly with " mediæval ", which was based on a different set of prerequisites that link it with the pre-classical civilization of the ancient East,[1] which resembled it in its non-rational, supernatural, and authoritarian character.

The modern epoch, which began with the Renaissance and with the commercial civilization that arose at the time of the great voyages of discovery in the fifteenth and sixteenth centuries, has

[1] Cf. *At the Cross-roads of History*, F. A. Ridley.

evolved steadily away from the supernatural and authoritarian civilization of the Middle Ages, and, as it has gained in strength and self-confidence, has more and more substituted secular—*i.e.* political—action for theological—*i.e.* supernatural—action. But, unlike the classical civilization of antiquity, which had only shadowy local cults to contend with, modern society, ever since its inception, has had to fight a continuous, uninterrupted battle against the surviving forces of mediæval civilization which have lingered on in its midst.

Of these forces, atavistic in the strictest sense of the term, the Roman Catholic Church was, and still is, by far the strongest. Indeed, at the end of the Middle Ages the power of the Church and of the supernatural order of thought which it embodied was so overwhelming that it was absolutely impossible to challenge it directly. Consequently, while individual free-thinkers existed at the epoch of the Reformation, they were not a force capable of making a direct attack upon either Church doctrine or Papal power.

It was only by disguising themselves under a religious cloak that individualism and " private judgement " could make their first breaches in the citadel of ecclesiastical modes of thought. Thus it was under the leadership of religious heresiarchs, Luther and Calvin, and not of the pantheist Giordano Bruno, or the rationalist Socinus, that the modern world made its first mass attack on the mediæval order of life.

This necessity for a religious disguise, which was not finally discarded until the French Revolution, furnished the most convincing evidence of the tremendous strength of mediæval Christianity and of its supreme embodiment, the Papacy. In its struggle against the mediæval Church modern civilization found its own feet, and, in its mature form, finally disclosed the secular character which had been implicit in it from the start.

The evolution of modern civilization from the religious to the secular, from theology to political action, can be clearly seen if we glance at the three great anti-traditional movements which have successively battered down the walls of mediæval society : the Protestant Reformation, the English Civil War, and the French Revolution.

The first of these was religious ; it fought under theological standards, and its leaders, Luther, Calvin, Zwingli, and Knox, were theologians who appeared before the world as the leaders of movements avowedly religious. The second, the English Revolution, was a hybrid movement, partly political and partly religious ; it represented both Puritanism and Parliament. Its leader, Oliver Cromwell, was a layman, but a lay preacher. The combination gives the history of the English revolution in a nutshell.

It was not until the late eighteenth century that the modern epoch finally shed its mediæval swaddling-clothes, and assumed its own distinctively original characteristics. The French Revolution was the first revolution which was entirely " modern " in character. It marked the end of the transitional era which formed the watershed between the religious and authoritarian civilization of the mediæval period, and the secular civilization of modern times, the era of science, of political democracy and individual rights.

It was, accordingly, the French Revolution which originated the crisis of Liberalism, the crisis of the nineteenth and early twentieth centuries, the fifth crisis of the Papacy according to the computation here adopted. [1]

A liberal historian of the present day sums up the situation created for the Papacy by the French Revolution and by the international liberal movement which dates its origins from that epoch-making event.

"So we are led to consider the ultimate antinomy which divides society in the Latin states of Europe. On the one hand there is the republican tradition dominant and established in France, evident, though overmastered, in Spain, partially transfused into the institutions of the national monarchy in Italy. On the other hand there is the Catholic church, the ally of the Bourbon who rules in Spain, and of the Bourbons who can never rule in France, and the enemy and the victim of the French Revolution. The gulf is clear, the incompatibility absolute, the war truceless. The old school of Gallicans, the later school of liberal Catholics, has died out. Ultramontanism has killed it, the thing itself and the bitter ultramontane journalists of the Empire who felt the sting of the Italian wars and spread the poison through France. The

[1] By "Liberalism" we understand throughout not merely a political movement, but a cultural philosophy, the mental outlook that pre-eminently characterized the nineteenth century.

syllabus of 1864 and the Infallibility decree of 1870 have cut away the hazy ' middle ground ' in which many a generous and divided soul found a reconciliation for his inner discords. A French child must either be brought up a Roman Catholic or he must be brought up a Republican. There is no real alternative. In the first case he will learn that the French Revolution was the crime of crimes, that divorce is a sin, that civil marriage is a sin, that monarchy is the best form of government, that liberty is an alias for wanton pride, and that with the exception of two brief interludes the whole history of France since 1789 has been one ghastly aberration from the path of godly duty. And in the second case he will learn just the opposite of all this, that the Church in all ages has been the enemy of human freedom and progress, that the Civil Code is the charter of social emancipation, and that the French Revolution was the discovery of social justice upon earth. The Third Republic has captured the schools, dissolved the congregations, and disestablished the Church, but it still rules over a divided nation." [1]

Such, in brief, was the situation in the era between the French and the Russian Revolutions, the epoch *par excellence* of Liberalism, which presented the Papacy with the fifth crisis in its history. Politically by its doctrine of democracy, economically

---

[1] N.B.—Recent events in Spain have extended the area of this contrast.

[1] H. A. L. Fisher, *The Republican Tradition in Europe*, (1911), pp. 253-254.

by its doctrine of Free Trade which battered down the Chinese Wall that cut off mediæval Christendom from the world, intellectually by the freedom of discussion and discovery to which it directly gave rise and to whose furtherance its institutions were pre-eminently adapted, and which resulted from its suppression of legal intolerance in the religious field, the liberal movement inaugurated by the era of revolutions which the great French Revolution began, challenged both the Papal power and the Catholic world philosophy at every point.

To the authority of the Middle Ages it opposed the freedom of modern discussion, to the static conception of life peculiar to a theological system " once for all delivered to the saints " it opposed the concept of evolution, which is logically fatal to every system that presupposes finality, to the supremacy of the ecclesiastical hierarchy and of its Papal head it opposed the liberal conception, ancient and modern, but never mediæval, of " the free Church in the free State ", a social conception which places the State at the centre of existence and the Church on the circumference.

Indeed, the fundamental antagonism between the liberal philosophy and the fundamental outlook of the Roman Catholic Church may be summarized in a sentence : the transference of the centre of human interest and authority from heaven to earth. To the liberal, this world represented reality, the next merely hypothesis. Between such a conception and the Catholic conception of life only war to the knife could conceivably exist.

As the modern world moved farther away from the world of the Middle Ages, its successive crises increased in severity. Even the crisis of the Reformation, which left the hull of religion intact and merely assaulted the superstructure of theological belief, did not challenge the Papacy nearly as fundamentally as did the liberal revolution. Henceforth, the Papal power represented a mediæval anachronism, even in the continent where it has so long borne sway. Between the alien worlds of mediæval and modern times peace was impossible; there could only be war.

If the Papacy should, by all the laws of evolution, have failed to survive in the revolutionary epoch of the sixteenth century, the epoch of Copernicus and Galileo, by so much the more should it have failed to survive in the far more drastically revolutionary nineteenth century, the era of Darwin and Marx, when not merely were its outworks threatened, but equally its elementary right, not merely to rule, but even to exist.

Yet in spite of all this the Papacy survived the nineteenth century, and endured as a world force, powerful and respected where it lingered on, the unfamiliar ghost of a bygone epoch. It has survived the last century, and visibly threatens to-day to outlive the Protestant churches of the Reformation, those relics of its earlier crisis, which but yesterday appeared destined to administer the *coup de grâce* to the ancient theocratic dynasty, the immortal " milk white hind " whom innumerable huntsmen have wounded, but whom none could kill.[1]

To-day storms roll up from the horizon which

[1] " A milk-white hind, immortal and unchang'd "—Dryden, *The Hind and the Panther*, referring to the Catholic Church.

threaten to engulf the liberal movements that but a short time back appeared to hold the centre of the European stage in perpetuity. Yet the Papacy still lives on. It now remains, in a brief investigation, to consider by what means it survived the perilous " century of stupendous progress ", a century so alien to it, and at whose doctrines, elsewhere regarded as self-evident, it hurled its most ferocious anathemas, before we pass on to consider in more detail the nature of the crisis of the present century which has succeeded the Liberal crisis, and threatens to engulf entirely the political, the ecclesiastical, and the intellectual institutions which have survived from the distant pre-scientific past into the alien atmosphere of the contemporary world.

Note O

" The whole of material and, likewise, mental life was dominated by the Church, which was interwoven with the whole life of the people, until in the course of time the ecclesiastical mode of thinking became a kind of instinct blindly followed like a natural law, and to act contrary to it was felt to be unnatural. All expressions of political, social, and family life were clothed in ecclesiastical forms, such thinking and behaving persisted long after the disappearance of the material causes which had produced them " ; Kautsky, *op. cit.*, p. 41.

(b) THE SOLUTION

By the middle of the seventeenth century, when the "World War" of Jesuitism, the Thirty Years' War, came to an end, the Catholic Counter-Reformation had spent its force. In the following century the Papacy appeared to succumb to the prevailing atmosphere of latitudinarian tolerance which characterized that epoch in general. As temporal princes the Popes intrigued with Protestant states, even playing, in this respect, an equivocal part in the Thirty Years' War itself. Pope Innocent XI endeavoured, for prudential reasons, to check the proselytizing zeal of Louis XIV of France and James II of England. In the eighteenth century we have the liberal Pope, Benedict XIV (1740-58), to whom the arch-freethinker, Voltaire, dedicated his play *Mahomet*, and of whom the atheist, Frederick the Great, spoke with marked respect. In 1773, as already remarked, the Jesuit order, the citadel of intransigence in the Roman Church, was dissolved by Pope Clement XIV on general grounds of Church policy. In fact, the latitudinarian Papacy of this century bore a very slight relationship to the fiercely ultramontane papacy of that which succeeded.

As we have already seen, the extraordinary vitality which has always been the outstanding characteristic of the Papal institution has never failed to manifest itself in its succeeding crises which have always evoked a strong reaction on the part of the Vatican. This perennial characteristic was again manifested at the outbreak of the French Revolution and the beginning of the liberal epoch which followed it.

In common with the other European rulers of the *ancien régime*, the Popes felt the heavy hand, first of the French Republic, then of Napoleon. For several years the Papal States formed part of Napoleon's kingdom of Italy, and its French possession of Avignon was permanently lost. Both Pius VI and his successor Pius VII were carried into exile, where the former died (1799). When, on the downfall of Napoleon in 1814, Pius VII returned to Rome, he immediately restored the Jesuit order, thereby inaugurating the nineteenth-century ultramontane movement, which culminated in the Vatican decree of Infallibility in 1870.

From 1814 to 1870 the Papacy was busily engaged in consolidating the Church in the face of the Liberal attack, and, for the achievement of this end, in establishing its own dictatorship in, and over, the Church. The process of hardening and narrowing the confines of Catholic dogma and its administrative counterpart, the Roman Curia, which had begun at the time of the Council of Trent, was now carried forward to its logical conclusion, the rigid centralization of all ecclesiastical authority in the hands of the Papacy, and the virtual establishment of a permanent dictatorship.

In its origin the ultramontane movement was merely one aspect of the autocratic reaction which followed upon, and formed the reply to, the revolutionary era.

It was no accident that Count de Maistre, whose book *Du Pape* (1820) may be said to have been

the first and completest expression of ultramontanism, was the minister of the King of Sardinia, the
friend of the Jesuits, at the court of Tsar Alexander
of Russia, the founder of " the Holy Alliance "
for the restoration and preservation of the *ancien
régime* in Europe by the combined military power
of Russia, Austria, and Prussia.

But, while the Holy Alliance has gone, and with
it the European conservatism of the early nineteenth century, the ultramontane movement
achieved an overwhelming victory within the Roman
Catholic Church, and still exercises a decisive
authority over it. [1]

In order to comprehend the real nature of the
transformation which the Roman Catholic Church
underwent in this century, it is necessary to realize
that the essential motives for its policy of extreme
centralization and Papal autocracy were social and
not theological in character. Ever since the Reformation that Church has been in a state of siege,
surrounded on every hand by an alien and un-
friendly world. Indeed, this essentially exclusive
character is what really divides the Church of pre-
Reformation times, which moved in easy mastery
through the world of mediæval civilization, from
modern Catholicism.

Moreover, ever since the Reformation, the
character of European civilization, and of the
revolutions which have successively moulded it,
has become more and more alien to the Church,
whose cultural philosophy has become more and
more an absolute anachronism in the modern
world. Consequently, we can express the essential

[1] See Note P, pp. 121-122.

nature of Catholic evolution since the Reformation, by remarking that it has increasingly adapted its institutions dating from an earlier age, to the conditions of the permanent state of siege which has been its actual rôle in modern times.

This process of internal militarization, for such, in effect, it was, was begun by the Jesuits and the Council of Trent in the mid-sixteenth century, and was completed in 1870 by the Vatican decree which riveted for ever upon the Roman Catholic Church the absolute power and doctrinal infallibility of the Pope.

Whereas in the crisis of the sixteenth century the chief part was actually played by the Jesuits, whose power virtually overshadowed that of the Popes, in the nineteenth the Jesuits, though active and influential, were subordinate to the Papacy itself. In fact, just as in a battle there must be a visible standard around which to rally the army, so the Roman Church, beleaguered on all sides by the liberal Revolution, required a central authority round which all could rally and which all could see ; such an authority could only be that of the Papacy.

A modern Roman Catholic historian has frankly admitted that, whatever theological arguments may have been used at the Vatican Council in order to justify the proclamation of the dogma of Papal Infallibility, the real motive that lay behind its proclamation was social and not theological in character. In his monograph on *The Papacy and Modern Times* the late Canon William Barry, himself an eye-witness of the Council, expressed the opinion that :

" On prelates like Manning, Martin, Bonne-
chose, Deschamps ; on laymen such as Veuillot
and Ward, it was borne in by the course of events
that to save society, spiritual authority must be
concentrated in the hands of the Pope, whom
all acknowledge as the highest representative
of Christian principles in the world.   These
writers had their own way of reasoning, no
doubt ; their moving impulse, however, was
quite as much a social necessity as a deduction
from grounds of doctrine, and its perfect expression was given by Joseph de Maistre, when
he published his treatise *Du Pape* after Napoleon's
downfall.   The Vatican Council was intended
to protect Catholic interests from anarchy by
completing the work begun at Florence and
left unfinished at Trent, of defining ' St Peter's
privileges ' in his successor . . . .

. . . . moreover, in the presence of a universal
dissolving movement, anti-social no less than
anti-Christian, a perpetual dictator was needed,
and who could it be, save the Pontifex Maxi-
mus ? " [1]

The last sentence in the above quotation sums
up the real situation in a nutshell.   But is it not
a trifle peculiar that a Roman Catholic theologian
should so naively admit that the fulfilment of the
promises made by Christ to Peter had to wait
seventeen centuries and a half before the French
Revolution arrived to implement them ?   At this
rate, the " social contract " and the Jacobin club,
which inaugurated the French Revolution and the

[1] Barry, *op. cit.*, pp. 245-6.

liberal epoch, formed indispensable links in the chain of Christian revelation.

The Vatican Decree, which did away with the last relics of constitutional government within the Catholic Church, cannot, in fact, be considered in isolation ; it must be taken in conjunction both with the famous *Syllabus of condemned Propositions*, issued by Pope Pius IX six years earlier, in 1864, and, also with the Papal cult, which throughout the generation prior to the Vatican Council had swelled to monstrous proportions.[1] The purely theological arguments used in support of the proclamation of Papal Infallibility were unusually weak, even for theological special pleading.

In fact, as late as 1832, the German, Adam Mohler, in his classical work on *Symbolism*, one of the most famous Roman Catholic theological works of the nineteenth century, not merely repudiated the concept of Papal Infallibility as unworthy of acceptance, but expressly stated that, *per se*, the infallibility of any individual apart from the Church was totally irreconcilable with the Catholic doctrine of the infallibility of the Church itself.[2] At the beginning of the nineteenth century a popular Roman Catholic Catechism used in England categorically stated that Papal infallibility was a Protestant calumny !

It is well known that Döllinger, the most learned Church historian of his day, preferred to endure excommunication rather than submit to the decree, which he regarded as quite unverifiable and contrary to Catholic tradition. Such arguments,

---

[1] See Note Q, p. 122.
[2] See Note R, p. 123.

however, serve only to demonstrate that the Papacy is far from being guided by purely theological considerations. It is, in fact, quite obvious that the motives which induced the Papacy to claim infallibility in 1870 rather than at some earlier date were due to the circumstances of the world of that time, a world which differed so sharply from that of earlier centuries.

If the theological arguments for the Vatican decrees were abysmally weak, the social and political arguments in its favour were overwhelmingly strong, and the Papacy is, and always has been, much more than a mere theological professorship. It has always been the paradox of Papal Imperialism that it must cloak its acts under a professedly theological guise in order to defend the vast array of vested interests with which it is associated.

Hence, to check the progress of the liberal Revolution and to exorcise even more crimson spectres to the Left, the Papacy had to shield itself behind the bulwark of infallibility, and, to assume this rôle, had to justify arguments against modern liberalism by citations from ancient scriptures, and to invoke the authority of the ancient Jewish fisherman, Peter, against the arguments of the modern Jewish agitators of the First International !

Stripped of theological verbiage, the " Syllabus " represented the answer of the Church militant to the militant battle-cries of the social revolution, and the Vatican decree marked the transformation of the Church into an ecclesiastical totalitarian state, in which the last vestiges of internal democracy were stilled for ever and the " leader " principle was firmly established in perpetuity.

H

Actually, the Papacy in 1870 already understood and adopted *in toto* the entire authoritarian principle of the counter-revolution acclimatized half a century later to the secular state under the generic title of Fascism. Ecclesiastical Fascism—as it may be termed —dates from that year. That the answer to social revolution is " Totalitarianism ", and a permanent dictatorship, was known to the Papacy for half a century before the secular reaction discovered it ; this constitutes a further proof of the perspicacity of the arch-reactionary of the modern world.

A contemporary Swiss historian thus summarizes the Papal measures of 1864 and 1870 :

" Pope Pius IX on his side showed his gratitude by pronouncing liberal revolutionary theories to be erroneous and forbidden by the Church. This attitude found its classic expression in the ' Syllabus of Modern Errors ' which the Pope issued with his Encyclical of December 8, 1864. This declared emphatically that society must be built up again on the basis of legitimate order, now that Catholic civilization had been weakened (note the sequence) by Lutheranism, Jansenism, Voltaireanism, and Socialism. The ' Syllabus ' therefore declared erroneous liberal principles which related directly to church matters like the right to freedom of worship, but also many of the fundamental demands of liberalism in general.

" Of still greater practical importance was the establishment of an unlimited supreme ower within the Catholic Church which took place a little later. It had always been a matter of dispute whether definitions of dogma could be made by the Pope alone, or whether they had to be confirmed by the sanction of the church, represented in ecclesiastical assemblies or councils. This was also a dispute between the authority of the national churches and that of the Pope; since the bishops, who formed the overwhelming majority at councils, were inevitably more or less dependent upon the State governments, the exclusion of Councils from control was equivalent to putting an end to what was left of the influence exercised by governments upon the central authority of the Catholic Church."

Having proceeded to point to the decisive victory then gained by the Pope at the Vatican Council, where no temporal governments were represented and the infallibility of the Pope, *apart from the Church*, was dogmatically affirmed, the author concludes :

" Thus the Catholic Church, also, as a bulwark against the International, had been able to strengthen itself as an international organization superior to national governments ; it offered itself as an ally, indeed, to the conservative states, but it was more independent of national governments than had hitherto been the case." [1]

The creation of the Papal dictatorship represents the answer of the Roman Catholic Church to the modern cultural revolution which was inaugurated in 1789 by the French Revolution, and subsequently spread throughout the leading centres of European civilization. But, in transforming

[1] Eduard Fueter, *World History* 1815-1920, pp. 226-227.

the Church into a permanent dictatorship, the Vatican Council manifested yet again that remarkable adaptability to changing circumstances which the Papacy has never failed to display. For the Infallibility Decree changed not merely the authority of the Church, but also the nature of that authority. Furthermore, in spite of the generally reactionary character of the Vatican Council, called together by Pius IX, a thorough-going reactionary in theology and (since the revolution of 1848) in politics, and dominated by such die-hard mediæval-ists as the ultramontane Cardinal Manning and the Jesuit Father Perrone, the Decrees altered the character of Papal authority, and altered it in a progressive manner, so as to meet the exigencies of an era of unprecedented rapidity of change. This fundamental transformation has escaped the notice of historians, but it may become of the greatest importance in the solution of the next great crisis of the Church, that of the twentieth century, in the midst of which we live to-day.

Prior to 1870, the infallibility of the Church in questions of morals and doctrine was universally accepted by all Catholic theologians as an article of faith. It was, however, the Church, and not any individual Pope or bishop, which exercised and transmitted the Divine revelation [1]—*i.e.*, the right to make, and to " interpret "—virtually to un-make dogma, lay in the " dead hand " of the Church, and was, as such, unchangeable ; since, obviously, tradition cannot change itself, and the General Councils of the Church only met at intervals of centuries. From the Council of Trent

[1] See Note R, p. 123.

to its successor at the Vatican, 306 years had elapsed (1564 ; 1870). Such a tradition could adapt itself only to a slowly moving age, to the stagnant agricultural civilization of the Middle Ages, not to the swiftly-moving civilization of modern times.

Had the Roman Catholic Church remained in this state, it must have petrified into the likeness of the Orthodox Churches of the East, which are, and always have been, entirely dominated by the dead hand, so that they can now survive only in an entirely unprogressive form, and instantaneously collapse when confronted by the successful forward movement of society.

In fact, if we would see what would actually be the inevitable fate of the Roman Church, had the Vatican decree not superseded the perpetual mortmain of tradition, we have only to look at the totally unprogressive, tradition-bound Russian Orthodox Church, which lacked any power of self-reformation, save from a Tsarist State as moth-eaten as itself, or a General Council, which no one possessed the power to call.

But for the Vatican Council, the collapse of the Roman Catholic Church before the intellectual and social revolutions of Europe in the present century would probably be as catastrophic as was that of the Russian Church before the social and intellectual revolution effected by the Bolsheviks in 1917. For the law of life is evolutionary change, and a system which will not bend will eventually break, even if it is infallible.

From this fate the Vatican decree, which transferred the power to make dogma (of course under the pretence of " revealing " it) from the dead

Church to the living Pope, from an unchanging
to a changing authority, was designed to save
the Roman Catholic Church by imparting to it the
power of change in accordance with the needs of a
changing epoch. As I have written elsewhere :

> " But in the doctrine of the infallibility of the
> living and changing Pope she (the Church)
> has an unrivalled instrument for going forward
> as well as back ! Attention has generally been
> drawn to the reactionary nature of this doctrine,
> but unless we greatly err, Rome will know how
> to go forward with this unrivalled instrument
> for ' liquidating the dead hand ' of the past
> for the development of doctrine and morals,
> and for adapting Romanism to tasks and
> problems which lay beyond the limited horizon
> of the Middle Ages. The Vatican Council of
> apparent reactionaries, who decreed this dogma
> in 1870, provided the church with a superb
> evolutionary weapon, equally adapted to re-
> actionary or progressive purposes." [1]

The theory of " development ", which thus
triumphed at the Vatican Council, had been lying
dormant for some time ; it had been first pro-
pounded by the Jesuit thinker, Denis Petau (or
Petavius) in the seventeenth century, when it fell
on barren ground, and it was revived by J. H.
Newman in his *Essay on the Development of Christian
Doctrine* (1845), one of the most remarkable works
on the philosophy of history that appeared during
last century. Newman laid down the revolutionary

[1] F. A. Ridley, *Marx, Aristotle, and the Black International*, " The
New Adelphi ", January, 1933.

postulate that " To live is to change ; to be perfect is to have changed often." [1] But Rome has a wonderful instinct for knowing what will serve her purpose, and in spite of the domination of the reactionary party in the Church, Newman not merely escaped condemnation, but was later made a Cardinal.

A doctrine of " development " was a *sine qua non* for the survival of the Church as a living force, and the fact that this was perceived by the reactionaries, who, in 1845 and long after, controlled the Church, must be regarded as one of the most remarkable proofs of foresight that even the Papacy has ever displayed.[2]

The ultimate significance of Newman's epoch-making work was discerned immediately by an acute contemporary critic. In a masterly passage the Protestant theologian, Isaac Taylor, thus expressed himself, twenty-one years before the Vatican Council, which he did not live to see :

" The lately-divulged doctrine of " development " would seem as if it had been now announced as the requisite preliminary to such a relinquishment of ancient practices and principles as we are supposing to be probable. It is manifest that if ' the Church ' be endowed with a creative or recreative vital energy, enabling and authorizing it, from age to age, to evolve what is new in belief, or in worship, or to bring to light what had previously slumbered in darkness ; if, for example, the church of the ninth century

---

[1] Newman, *op. cit.,* 1878 edition, p. 40.
[2] See Note S, pp. 123-124.

ought to be thought of as an authentic product of the church of the third, although marked by new features—then this same vital force, this power of adaption, may, as ages roll on, and as human reason ripens, show its energies in the mode of absorption or retrenchment. During the ninth century, the Church put forth a verdant top, darkening all the skies, but in the nineteenth century the tree may call in its sap from its luxurious head, while it strikes its roots far into a new soil.

" If, in this age of reason, certain dogmas or modes of worship may seem to have fulfilled their intention, and to have become encumbrances rather than aids, why may not the inherent ' development ' power rescind, withdraw, remove such adjuncts ? It is not easy to see what difficulty, either logical or theoretic, stands in the way, to prevent the Church's faculty of development from now shifting its position, and acting as a faculty of abrogation. Once it put its right hand forth to bring from its treasury things new, henceforward it will be putting out its left hand to withdraw these worn and faded articles from their places. In a rude age the Church—always wise in her day—became flagrantly polytheistic ; in a philosophic, or rather a scientific, age, the same church, equally wise, will become pantheistic." [1]

The striking prophecy quoted above received a remarkable confirmation at the Vatican Council, which first condemned the " anti-Christian " theory

[1] Isaac Taylor, *Ignatius Loyola*, pp. 325-326.

of " progress " and then tacitly restored to the Church her power to move with the times. When Pius IX made the profound observation,—universally misconstrued by his liberal critics—" I am tradition ", he summed up the silent revolution which the decree of Papal infallibility had effectually accomplished. Henceforth, the " Leader " principle was dogmatically accepted in the Roman Catholic Church in all its implications ; truth and tradition become the will of the Papal leader, who is not guided by the dead hand of the past, but by the living needs of the present. The motto ascribed to Galileo : " It moves all the same ", was now adopted by the Papacy which had condemned him.

Armed with this supremely flexible authority, the Papacy survived the liberal crisis of the nineteenth century, and moved forward into the twentieth to face the all-embracing crisis which agitates the world of to-day.

It is, accordingly, to this contemporary crisis as it affects the Papacy, and to the Papal solution of this crisis which threatens that ancient institution as it has never been threatened before, that the second and third parts of this book will be devoted, now that an attempt has been made to place the Papacy's present crisis in that proper perspective which a study of its earlier crises alone is capable of providing.

Note P : *Restoration of the Jesuits*

" I am persuaded that the Jesuits alone are able to defy a revolution. As I am resolved to use my last man and my last coin to crush the revolution, it follows that I give the Jesuits liberty of action in my territories." (Victor Emmanuel I of Sardinia and Savoy in 1815). This may be said to sum up in a sentence the essential rôle of the Jesuits in the era of the restoration.

Note Q : The Cult of the Pope

"Before 1848", writes the Old Catholic, von Schulte, who can speak from his own experience, "the Pope was only mentioned in schools when absolutely necessary. Before 1848 I never heard a sermon about the States of the Church or anything similar. But since 1848 more sermons have been preached about them in many places than about the Gospel." In England where, after 1853, an organized hierarchy once more existed, people began to talk about "devotion to the Pope". "The Sovereign Pontiff", said the Oratorian Faber in a sermon, "is the third visible presence of Jesus Christ among us, the visible Head of the Church in the Blessed Sacrament." The Latin countries went even further than Germany and England. It is enough to recall what occurred in France, and the language of the agitator Louis Veuillot, whose journal, *L' Univers*, became the mouthpiece of ultramontane aspirations. Peculiar zeal was shown by the Jesuits under the leadership, after 1853, of the Belgian, Pierre Jean Beckx, "the Black Pope". The *Civiltà Cattolica*, founded in 1850 in Naples and shortly after transferred to Rome, became the principal organ of their new journalism, intended for the laity as well as the clergy. This paper soon won the special favour of the Pope, who found in it sentences like the following: "When the Pope thinks, it is God who thinks in him" (cf. Gustav Krüger, *The Papacy*, pp. 235 and 236).

Note R

"To no individual, considered as such, doth infallibility belong, for the Catholic, as is clear from the preceding observations, regards the individual only as a member of the whole, as living and breathing in the Church. When his feelings, thoughts and will are conformable to her spirit, then only can the individual attain to inerrability. Were the Church to conceive the relation of the individual to the whole in an opposite sense, and consider him as personally infallible, then she would destroy the very notion of community; for communion can only be conceived as necessary, when the true faith and pure and solid Christian life cannot be conceived in individualization."[1]

Note S

It has been sometimes suggested that Newman's *Development* anticipated Darwin's later work, the *Origin of Species* (1859). There is, however, a world of difference between "evolution" and "development". The first is as incompatible with revelation and dogmatic Christianity as the second is compatible with them. "Evolution"

[1] Cf. Adam Möhler, *Symbolism* (1832), vol. II. p. 10.

presupposes that *everything* changes, foundation equally with the superstructure built upon it. "Development", on the other hand, presupposes change in the superstructure *built upon an unchanged foundation*. (Cf. Newman, *op. cit.*, p. 40. "It changes in order to remain the same.")

Cardinal Newman so interpreted his doctrine, and that subtle, and up to a point daring, thinker has never been condemned by Rome. But when some of his "Modernist" followers advanced beyond "development" to genuine "evolution", *i.e.* when they denied the permanent *basis* of Christianity and revelation, they were necessarily, condemned by Rome, *e.g.* the Abbé Loisy's *L'Évangile et l'Église*, which denies the finality even of the Gospel. Of course, no believer in a fixed and final revelation can logically be an evolutionist, certainly not a Pope! (Cf. Rev. J. A. Zahm, *Evolution and Dogma*. The reverend author does not, however, consider the effect of the evolutionary doctrine—which he professes to reconcile with dogma—on the Christian revelation itself.)

PART TWO

THE PAPACY AND THE CRISIS OF THE TWENTIETH CENTURY

INTRODUCTION

THE crisis which confronts the Papacy in the twentieth century cannot be considered as, in any sense, an isolated phenomenon. The progress of modern civilization, in all its branches, from authority to reason, has been a continuous one ever since the recovery of European civilization from the cultural eclipse of the Dark Ages which followed the passing of the Graeco-Roman civilization in Western Europe, disguised as it often was under the cloak of religious heresy ; no one who attentively surveys the evolution of European civilization since the thirteenth century can avoid the conclusion that the whole process has been one which continuously and in ever-increasing measure has shifted its centre of gravity from religious authority to human experience.

Increasingly, the tendency of Western civilization, from the age of Frederick Hohenstaufen to that of the " anti-God " campaigns of contemporary Soviet Russia, has been to relegate authority derived from the supernatural to the circumference of civilization, and in its stead to instal the authority of human reason, human knowledge, and human experience.

We say that this has been the " tendency " of modern civilization, and we use the word advisedly, not forgetting a modern philosopher's classical definition of this word.[1]   The course of European civilization from authority to reason has been by no means an uninterrupted one ; far from this being the case, rationalism—using the word in its widest and most comprehensive sense—has had to fight every step of the way, with innumerable setbacks and countless martyrs, opposed as it has been by vested interests at every step, and, in the religious field, above all by the arch-reactionary, the Roman Catholic Church.

For the Papacy, old, and deeply versed in human affairs, has no illusions as to the ultimate fate which must befall it if and when it is pushed by the advance of modern reason from the centre of the stage to the remotest rim of the social periphery Consequently it has always fought to the end against such a fate.   It always will and must fight to the end against it.   *Semper eadem*, " For ever the same " now as in the past it confronts the crisis of the twentieth century, as it confronted the preceding crises in its long and battle-strewn history, resolved, come what may, to exist, and resolved to fight its secular foes to the bitter end. Our preceding sketch of its earlier reactions to its successive crises does not warrant any belief, either in its present incapacity to fight back when the occasion demands, or in any reasonable probability that it will vanish " softly and silently ", without a struggle, from the scene.

For if the crisis of this century, which marks and witnesses the birth-pangs of a new, wholly

---

[1] Tendency, *i.e.*, a law whose absolute execution is checked by countervailing circumstances, or is by them retarded or weakened. Karl Marx, *Das Kapital*, Vol. III, p. 215 of German edition.

rational world, threatens in passing to sweep away all ancient landmarks, not least does it threaten the oldest and most atavistic of them all, the Church of Rome, venerable before modern civilization was thought of, and reactionary already before the modern doctrine of " progress " had been formulated even by the boldest of human thinkers.

The crisis of our century, which to-day confronts the Papacy, is the heir and residuary legatee of all the earlier crises in its history ; it includes and transcends them all. It unites and gathers into one the science of the Arabs, the " private judgement " of the reformers, the scepticism of the Renaissance, and the scientific enlightenment of the eighteenth and nineteenth centuries. It extends science, and this is its most novel and dangerous feature, from the investigation of inorganic nature to the social inheritance of mankind. It thereby drives religion from the last vestige of supernaturalism, the dark undergrowths of human society wherein social misery has so long nourished human faith.

If the successive crises of earlier ages cut down the superabundant foliage that grew in tropical luxuriance on the tree of the supernatural, the present crisis will, if unchecked, track the very origins of religious belief to their source in the diseased roots of human society and then proceed to make an end of them altogether.

Religion, and particularly the religion that is most rooted in the dark unconscious of the past, is threatened to-day, not with reformation, but with extinction, with relegation to the museum of prehistoric curiosities, and its passing would of necessity drag down the institutions which have grown up in its shadow, and which, though much of their activity may appear to have little to do with religion properly so called, could not possibly survive it, once the anchor of revelation had been forcibly torn from the depths of the human consciousness.

For, unlike the more modern forms of Christianity which have grown up alongside of liberalism, and willy-nilly partake of its spirit, Rome stands for a conception of supernatural religion elsewhere dead in the world of western civilization, the conception of a theocracy on which not merely is this world a mere training-ground for the next, but morals, government, culture, in a word all the essential activities of mankind, centre round the church and are ultimately subject to Catholic dogma and to the Roman Pontiff. It is as evident as anything can well be that such a conception of civilization and of the conditions of civilized existence is the very antithesis, the absolute negation, of the social philosophy of our times.

The keen historical sense that the conditions of its existence have instilled into the Papacy enables the Roman Curia to appraise the present crisis in the light of the broad perspectives afforded by its earlier crises. We remember the sequence of adversaries enumerated in the syllabus of 1864 as the successive enemies of the Church, socialism and secularism succeeding to the Reformation and to the liberal " enlightenment " as the prime foes of the Church. As will be demonstrated in the sequel, the Church can only destroy secularism and socialism, its leading opponents to-day, if it can at the same time annihilate the earlier philosophies, of which, whether it recognizes them or not, the revolutionary philosophy of political and cultural rationalism is now the heir.

To prevail in, and over, the twentieth century Rome must annihilate not merely her present antagonists in the modern crisis, but, equally and at the same time, her antagonists of bygone days, in so far as they still survive into this century. Liberalism, the progenitor of Socialism, Criticism, the parent of Rationalism, Science, the begetter of Secularism, all must perish in a common cultural *auto da fé*, in a comprehensive bonfire of the ages, if Rome is to surmount this crisis, the all-inclusive continuation of the earlier crises already enumerated.

Fortunately for Rome, there is, as will be shown later, a secular ally available which, albeit for somewhat different reasons, is under a similar obligation to make a holocaust of the political and cultural treasures of the past. Indeed, as we shall strive to make clear, the golden thread that binds together Romanism and Fascism in their reactions to the world and to the crisis of to-day, is the bond of an iconoclastic atavism that, in order to achieve the triumph of either the Rome of the Vatican or that of Mussolini, requires equally urgently the complete and irrevocable ruin of the rationalist civilization of modern times.

But before the Papal reaction to the crisis of the twentieth century is indicated and analyzed, we must glance at the main features of that crises just as we have done previously at the crises that preceded and led up to it. The second part of this study is directed to an examination of the crisis considered in its principal features, and the third part to the solution whereby the Papacy will seek to escape from and to triumph over it, as she has hitherto succeeded in escaping from and triumphing over its prototypes. For "*Semper eadem*" remains the watchword of the Papacy now, in the twentieth century, as in those that preceded it.

Chapter I

THE CRISIS OF THE TWENTIETH CENTURY

" Socialism is a consistent world philosophy, expressing itself as Communism in economics, Republicanism in politics, and Atheism in Religion."—August Bebel.

The crisis which now confronts the Papacy may be briefly described as the crisis of Socialism. Just as the outstanding enemy of the Roman Catholic Church in the sixteenth Century was Protestantism, and in the nineteenth Liberalism, so to-day, it is collectivism, under the alternative designations of Communism or Socialism, that confronts the Catholic Church as its pre-eminent and irreconcilable foe.

The Papacy, as its whole history serves to demonstrate, possesses an unerring urge to self-preservation, besides a keen sense of the drift of contemporary history. There is, therefore, nothing accidental in the central position accorded to the Socialist-Communist menace in the Papal pronouncements of the present generation. Rome has never wasted her ecclesiastical ammunition on enemies who were not really dangerous. She does not waste it to-day.

As we have already seen, the " Syllabus of Condemned Propositions ", issued as far back as 1864, had already enumerated Socialism as the final term and climax of the successive antagonists who have assailed the Church in modern times; we recall the sequence " Lutheranism, Voltaireanism (*i.e.* Liberalism) and Socialism ". Nor can there be any doubt that the Papal genealogist has stated the family relationship correctly. Liberalism was, beyond doubt, the child and authentic heir of the Reformation, without whose twin dogmas of individualism and private judgement the essential prerequisites of the Liberal epoch in human history would have been lacking. Similarly, there can be no doubt that the demand for economic and cultural democracy which constitutes the driving force behind contemporary Socialism would equally be impossible, had it not been for the political democracy and social and educational equality, which formed the core of the Liberal Revolution throughout its heyday in the last two centuries.

The fact that to-day Socialism, and still more Communism, profess the most vehement contempt for their Liberal precursors and their surviving relics, no more disproves this genealogy than the jeers, which the men of the eighteenth century " enlightenment " directed against the fanaticism of the reformers, disprove the contention that mankind could not have reached the Liberal era or arrived at the stage of political and intellectual revolt which the advent of modern Liberalism expressed and reflected without first passing through the religious revolution.[1]

The crisis of the twentieth century, the crisis pre-eminently, of Socialism, cannot, then, be considered in isolation as anything new in the crisis-racked history of the Papacy. The contemporary crisis takes its place beside and in succession to, the earlier crises in Papal history : and of such

[1] See Note T, pp. 162-3.

crises it is the sixth, according to the computation here adopted. As such it presents, as its predecessors presented, a problem which, again as in former days, the Papacy must solve under pain of extinction. It remains, accordingly, to state the essential terms of this crisis before considering what solution, if any, offers itself to the Papacy as a way of escape from the perils which confront it.

Broadly speaking, we may say that the victory of Socialism would of necessity be absolutely fatal to Roman Catholic Christianity and to the Papacy, whether we consider it from a practical or a theoretical standpoint. In practice, a Socialist State would be a self-sufficient society ; *it would leave no room for the Church*, *i.e.*, it would be a society completely materialistic, in the sense that it would know of no other forces than those at work in human society and in that realm of inanimate nature, wherefrom, according to materialist philosophy, human society originates, and whereby it is on every side surrounded.

From the standpoint of any supernatural philosophy of life, such as is pre-eminently that of Catholicism, the Socialist State, existing solely in and for humanity, would represent the very quintessence of secularism, of a society which not so much denied as ignored the supernatural. From this standpoint, every form of Socialism, and not only the openly materialist Marxist school, is equally anathema. If Protestantism curtailed the domain of the supernatural, and Liberalism politely releagted it to the province of the optional adjuncts of life—" the free Church in the free State "—the Socialist society warns it off the premises of human life altogether; its effective motto is: "The proper study of mankind is man."

From its own standpoint, therefore, the Papacy is quite right in regarding any form of Socialism as incompatible with the world-philosophy whose domination is the necessary prelude to its own existence and power. Indeed, the attitude of the Roman Catholic Church in openly opposing Socialism itself demonstrates that it, alone among the Christian Churches, retains both a definite philosophy and an autonomous vitality.

That Socialism and Catholicism can no more be mixed than fire and water, that they represent absolutely opposite and completely irreconcilable principles, that, in brief, Socialism is THE enemy, has long been obvious to the Papacy and has repeatedly been reaffirmed by it. Thus, on the eve of the revolution of 1848, when the modern proletariat first appeared as a political force, with Socialism as a distinct aim, Pope Pius IX (1846-78) declared:

"Communism is completely opposed to the natural law itself, and its establishment would entail the complete destruction of all property and even of human society" (Sept. 11, 1846).

The two great Papal Encyclicals which are landmarks in the struggle of the Papacy against its new enemy, Socialism, are equally denunciatory and explicit.

In his famous encyclical *Rerum Novarum*, of May 15, 1891, Pope Leo XIII (1878-1903) thus expressed himself:

" The practice of all ages has consecrated the principle of private ownership ", and concludes : " Hence it is clear that the main tenet of Socialism, community of goods, must be utterly rejected, since it would only injure those whom it would seem meant to benefit, is directly contrary to the rights of mankind, and would introduce confusion and disorder into the commonweal. The first and most fundamental principle, therefore, if one would undertake to alleviate the condition of the masses, must be the inviolability of private property."

The teachings of Pope Leo XIII have been modernized, but confirmed, by his ablest successor. In his encyclical *Quadragesimo Anno* (*i.e.*, " in the 40th year " after the encyclical of Leo XIII quoted above), Pope Pius XI (1922) again defines the essential antagonism that exists between all forms of Socialism and the Roman Catholic Church :

" Since the days of Pope Leo XIII, Socialism too, the great enemy with which his battles were waged, has undergone profound changes, no less than economics. At that time Socialism could be fairly termed a single system which defended certain definite and coherent doctrines. Nowadays it has in the main become divided into two opposing and often bitterly hostile camps, neither of which, however, has abandoned the principle peculiar to Socialism, namely, opposition to the Christian Faith."

(After enumerating the principal points which divide revolutionary communism from the more

moderate forms of reformist socialism, Pius XI
then pronounces officially upon the question
whether it is possible for a socialist of any kind
or under any circumstances to be a Christian
and a member of the Roman Catholic Church.)

"Whether Socialism be considered as a
doctrine or as an historical fact, or as a movement, if it really remains Socialism, it cannot be
brought into harmony with the dogmas of the
Catholic Church, even after it has yielded to
Truth and Justice in the points We have mentioned, the reason being that it conceives human
society in a way utterly alien to Christian truth.

"For according to Christian doctrine, man,
endowed with a social nature, is placed here on
Earth in order that he may spend his life in
society, and under an authority ordained by
God ; that he may develop and evolve to the
full his faculties to the praise and glory of his
Creator, and by fulfilling faithfully the duties of
his station, he may attain to temporal and eternal
happiness. Socialism, on the contrary, entirely
ignorant of, or unconcerned about, this sublime
end both of individuals and of society, affirms
that living in community was instituted merely
for the sake of the advantages which it brings
to mankind."

"Hence," concludes Pope Pius XI, ' Religious
Socialism ', ' Christian Socialism ', are expressions implying a contradiction in terms. No one
can be at the same time a sincere Catholic and a
true Socialist." (*Quadragesimo Anno*, May 15,
1931.)

It is self-evident from the above pronouncement —a pronouncement, it may be added, almost certainly on Catholic principles infallible—that the Papacy is under no illusions as to its irreconcilable opposition to Socialism, i.e. to the essential principle of the twentieth century, which WHEREVER IT REMAINS PROGRESSIVE tends as naturally towards Socialism as the progressive forces of the preceding century tended towards Liberalism. Indeed, this historic succession of Socialism to Liberalism is explicitly recognized by Pius XI, who adds, in the foregoing encyclical :

"Let all bear in mind that the parent of this cultural Socialism is Liberalism, and that its offspring will be Bolshevism." [1]

The essential opposition in nature between Catholicism and any society organized politically on Socialist lines is thus lucidly expressed by the ablest of recent Catholic writers to deal with this question ; it may be added that his references to Bolshevism would apply equally to any other society founded upon Socialist principles :

"Toleration and regard for tradition are alien to Bolshevism. It possesses a very definite philosophy of history, to whose fulfilment its State and economic experiments must minister. This philosophy finds the goal of humanity in the self-sufficient society. Bolshevism is thus essentially and wholeheartedly intolerant of Christianity and the Church. It cannot therefore

[1] See Note U, p. 163.

allow the Church to work freely within its
society and State; in this respect its attitude
is far more logical than that of the bourgeois
State. It aims at the complete identification
of public life and private belief. It is social
atheism." [1]

Social atheism! There, lucidly summarized, we
have the essential feature of Socialist society
vis-à-vis the Catholic Church philosophy. Indeed,
it would be hardly possible to improve upon
" social atheism " as an epitome of the crisis of
the twentieth century as it confronts the Papacy.
For " social atheism "—the complete extension of
secularism to the whole of society—expresses the
essential aim of Socialism and the essential objective
of that crisis, the conclusion and culmination of
the age-long movement of modern society from
the supernatural to the natural, from authority to
reason, from theocracy to complete humanism,
wherein Gods are banished from the human
commonwealth, and man himself becomes " the
master "—and sole measure—" of things ". It is
in this sense that the crisis of the twentieth century
not merely succeeds, but includes, all the preceding
crises; the State of Luther, which denied the
Real Presence, is succeeded by the State of Lenin,
which denies that there is any Presence to be Real !
Socialism thus presents itself to the Papacy as
the complete secularization of society, as the
absolute negation of the theocratic conception of
human existence of which Rome is the last great
champion in the West, as the culmination and

[1] Waldemar Gurian, *Bolshevism—Theory and Practice*, pp. 255-6.

completion of the "revolt of reason" which, ever since the close of the Dark Ages, has increasingly menaced Catholicism with destruction. Between Catholicism and Socialism no *via media* is now possible. For while it is possible for Protestantism to seek a compromise, and even to toy with the illusion of "Christian Socialism", this is impossible for Rome, since the essential feature of the Papacy, which is at once its strength and its weakness, is its attachment to first principles, upon which, however accommodating in non-essentials, she can never compromise.

In a theocratic conception of civilization, such as that of Papal Rome, the "unity of theory and practice" is evident and indissoluble. Her politics proceed from her world philosophy, and *vice versa*. It is obvious at a glance that not merely does Socialism threaten her existence on the practical field, but that it also, like Catholicism, but unlike Liberalism, possesses first principles which likewise require a unity of theory and practice that threatens Roman theory equally with Roman practice. Modern Communism cannot be conceived apart from its materialist philosophy of history, and it is evident that this is as diametrically opposed to the Catholic theory as the secular State of Socialism, its practical expression, is to the Papacy as a social force in the actual world.

That the Socialist theory of history, from which the Materialism that is its practice directly springs, is utterly irreconcilable with that of Catholicism, or, indeed, with any philosophy based on revelation, is evident to anyone who merely studies the barest outline of its nature in the works of the classical masters of Socialism; it is, consequently, sufficient to cite their *obiter dicta* on the subject. It may be added that the materialistic doctrines of the Marxist school are common, in this respect, to the non-Marxist schools of Socialism and Anarchism. In fact, wherever Socialism rises to a consciousness of its existence as a separate political force, it accepts the materialist conception of history as its essential basis.

What is Historical Materialism in essence? the world philosophy of International Socialism. It cannot be better described than in the words of its founders, Karl Marx (1818-83) and Fredrick Engels (1820-95); Engels thus characterizes the philosophy of which, along with Marx, he was the co-founder:

"By it, History for the first time was placed on its real foundation; the obvious fact, hitherto totally neglected, that first of all men must eat, drink and have shelter and clothing and therefore work, before they can struggle for supremacy or devote themselves to politics, religion, philosophy, etc.—this fact at last found historical recognition."[1]

i.e., the beginning, aim and end of human life and human society are to be found on earth, and are to be explained solely with reference to its conditions of existence. This fact is made even clearer by Karl Marx:

"The religious reflex of the real world can in any case only finally vanish, when the practical

[1] F. Engels, *Socialism Utopian and Scientific*.

relations of everyday life offer to man none but perfectly intelligible and reasonable relations with regard to his fellow-men and to nature.

" The life process of society, which is based on the process of material production, does not strip off its mystical veil until it is treated as production by freely associated men, and is consciously regulated by them in accordance with a settled plan.

" This, however, demands for society a certain material groundwork or set of conditions of existence which in their turn are the spontaneous product of a long and painful process of development." [1]

Hence, from the Marxian standpoint, now generally accepted throughout modern Socialism, the actual role of religion in modern Society is that succinctly emphasized by Marx in the following words :

" Religion is the soul of soulless conditions, the heart of a heartless world, the opium of the people. The suppression of religion as the happiness of the people is the revendication of its real happiness. The invitation to abandon illusions regarding its situation is an invitation to abandon a situation which has need of illusions. Criticism of religion is therefore the germ of a criticism of the vale of tears, of which religion is the holy aspect." [2]

[1] Marx, *Capital*, Vol. I.
[2] Marx, *Criticism of the Hegelian Philosophy of Law.*

A modern Socialist writer thus tersely sums up the bearing of historical Materialism, the world philosophy of Socialism, in its relationship to religion :

" No man can be consistently both a Socialist and a Christian. It must be either the Socialist or the religious principle that is supreme, for the attempt to couple them equally betrays charlatanism, or lack of thought. So surely does the acceptance of Socialism lead to the exclusion of the supernatural, that the Socialist has little need for such terms as Atheist, Freethinker or even Materialist ; for the word Socialist, rightly understood, implies one who on all such questions takes his stand on positive science, explaining all things by purely natural causation ; Socialism being not merely a politico-economic creed, but also an integral part of a consistent world philosophy." [1]

Such, in brief, is the world outlook of modern Socialism, already officially accepted in Russia, and widely diffused throughout the world ; a view, it should be repeated, accepted by all Socialist parties outside the British Isles, where, alone, Socialism has not yet assumed an anti-religious form. The Papacy has never condemned the moderate, non-Marxian Socialism of the British Labour Party. It represents a point of view accepted by Socialists and Anarchists, equally with the adherents of the Third (Communist) International, which, until

[1] *Socialism and Religion,* an anonymous pamphlet published by the Socialist Party of Great Britain, 2nd ed. (1925), p. 46.

recently, carried on a militant agitation against religion, on a world-wide scale, from the time of the Russian Revolution onwards.[1] A glance at this philosophy is sufficient to demonstrate that, if Socialism in practice means the end of the Papacy as an institution, Socialism in theory means the irrevocable end of the elaborate dogmatic system which forms the basis of the Roman Catholic religion.

For, as already observed, while the Roman Church can admit " development "—the internal development of her own doctrine on the basis of its fixed foundations—she cannot possibly accept " Evolution "—the idea that *everything* evolves, and that, therefore, religious and moral doctrines are no more fixed and final than anything else ; still less can she admit an evolutionary conception, such as the basic conception of Socialism, which is entirely materialistic in outlook, takes no account of any forces except the material, and indeed, does not recognize even the possibility that non-material forces exist.

It is therefore evident that, in the field both of thought and action, there is and must be war to the knife between Roman Catholicism and Socialism ; and that the crisis of the twentieth century, the crisis pre-eminently of Socialism, can only be solved in favour of the Church by means of the destruction of Socialism.

Broadly speaking, we may say that the universal prevalence of Socialism would mean the certain, and probably the rapid, extinction of religion,

---

[1] See Michael Bakunin, *God and the State*, for the views of Anarchism on Religion, which are much the same as those of Socialism.

which could hardly survive so drastic a change as would be involved in the transformation of the anarchic and fear-haunted chaos, which is present day " society ", into a world society as completely rational and scientific in all its departments as that of International Socialism, in which fear, ignorance and social misery, hitherto the great bulwarks of the supernatural, would have completely disappeared. On this point, indeed, a French Socialist aptly remarks :

" There can be no doubt that the Socialist atmosphere will speedily prove fatal to the Church. . . . When economic servitude is at an end, and when the right to work or to public assistance has become a reality for all, the Churches will be deserted. All the more will this ensue, seeing that even sincere believers do not seek the illusory comforts of religion except on account of the material and moral trials of their lives. But well-being, security, and the disappearance of the sufferings that are due to the defective organization of society, will render it needless to appeal any longer to a chimerical support from on high." [1]

If, in short, " Fear was the cause of religion ", as the old Epicurean poet-philosopher declared, Socialism, which will finally end, not indeed individual misery altogether, for such a promise would be clearly Utopian, but at least, preventable social misery, will simultaneously cut the roots of religion, and end the epoch which has been the

[1] Lucien Deslineres, *The Coming of Socialism*, p. 37.

epoch of religion. Hence, the Socialist solution of the crisis of the twentieth century would mark, if not the end, at least the beginning of the end, of religion.

Seeing that this is indubitably so, and that the materialistic doctrine of Socialism is irreconcilable with any form of supernatural religion, it might be supposed that every form of Christianity would unite against a doctrine whose definite triumph would sooner or later mean the end of that creed. But in actual practice this is not so. In fact, while isolated acts of opposition in the Protestant Churches have not been unknown, their general tendency has been to effect a compromise with Socialism, and "Christian Socialism" has been a recognized school of thought in all these bodies, particularly the Protestant Churches of England and America.

That the Roman Catholic Church has alone come out as the irreconcilable enemy of Socialism is due to the fact that she, alone among the contemporary Churches of Western Europe, is genuinely mediævalist—that is, she alone retains the conception of a theocracy—of a Church that is not merely an adjunct to human life and civilization, but its centre and master.

Consequently, the Roman Catholic Church alone, under the guidance of the living Pope, neither stares at Socialism with eyes blindfolded by dead tradition, as do the moribund Eastern Churches, nor seeks to reconcile the irreconcilable—Socialism with Christianity—by well-timed opportunism, as do those essentially opportunist institutions, the Protestant Churches. On the contrary, she comes out openly, equipped with a world philosophy as definite, distinct and uncompromising as that of Socialism itself; one similarly based on first principles, which she opposes in theory as in action to the antagonistic world-creed of Socialism.

The Papacy no more shrinks from the crisis of the twentieth century than it shrank from those that preceded it. Far from so doing, it is resolved to survive and to triumph over Marx and Lenin, as it has already triumphed over, and survived, their predecessors, Frederick Hohenstaufen and Galileo, Luther and Calvin, Voltaire and Rousseau. In the twentieth century, as for so long before, *Semper eadem*—" For ever the same "—remains its motto.

The outstanding characteristic of the Papacy may be described as " progressive continuity " —*i.e.*, it remains in essence what it has always been, yet manages to display flexibility and adaptability in relation to the needs of successive epochs. While, however, it was possible for the Papacy to adapt itself to the conditions of the slow-moving eras of the pre-industrial past, it is much harder to do so to-day in view of the headlong pace of modern life.

Hence, as in the realm of practical affairs, so also in the intellectual domain, Rome is forced by the course of modern development to take up her stand upon a world philosophy that is in sharpest contradiction to the essential concepts of modern thought. In spite of all that appearance of modernity which she has known so well how to assume, she remains bound to the conception of theocracy; she cannot divorce absolutism in practice from absolutism in thought. Consequently the Papacy still faces the modern world clad in the intellectual armour of the thirteenth century, the highest intellectual point which she reached before European civilization broke from its scholastic bed and rushed into the secular channels along which it has since flowed.

Ever since Leo XIII's Encyclical, *Aeterni Patris*, (August 4, 1879) which took up the challenge of modern thought by proclaiming an indissoluble alliance between the Roman Church and the scholastic philosophy of mediæval times, the Papacy has faced the modern world like some vast prehistoric monster, like some extinct Leviathan of the Saurian era clad in unwieldy armour of impenetrable thickness. In the age of Einstein and Freud, as in the preceding age of Darwin and Marx, the Church still maintains its spiritual alliance with the mediæval Normans, and opposes the mediæval intellectual world to that of modern times, the thirteenth century to the twentieth century; the age of the Crusades, wherein the scholastic philosophy first originated, to the age of radio and television. [1]

We can measure the anachronism involved when we consider that the mediæval knights of that military genius, William the Conqueror, would not last for five minutes on a modern battlefield against present-day science, but that nevertheless, according to Pope Leo XIII and his successors, the scholastic philosophy, whose founder was William's Archbishop, Lanfranc of Canterbury, is still competent to dominate the illimitable intellectual

[1] See Note V, p. 164.

universe of to-day! The comparison affords an accurate measure of the enormous gulf that separates the theocratic universe of the Papacy from the actual world in which we live.

From the time of the *Aeterni Patris* of Leo XIII, the Papacy has committed the Church to the task, impossible if modern civilization is to continue, of preserving intact the philosophy which summed up in a manner consonant with Catholic dogma the closed universe of mediæval times. A glance at this intellectual system suffices to disclose its absolute incompatibility with the evolutionary universe of modern knowledge. In the intellectual world, as in that of practical affairs, the destruction of modern civilization is a necessity if the Papacy is to survive.

For Thomas Aquinas, who was a reactionary even in the thirteenth century, the era of Frederick Hohenstaufen and Roger Bacon, cannot be progressive in the twentieth, the epoch *par excellence* of expanding and ubiquitous science. No more than his Papal protectors can Thomas Aquinas hope to teach our civilization, but, like them, *he can hope to survive it*.

The scholastic or "Thomist" philosophy was the answer of the Papacy to the crisis of the thirteenth century, the crisis of the recovery of European civilization in the epoch of the Crusades.[1] Its basic constituents were the dogmatic system of the Catholic Church and as much of Greek philosophy (mostly in Arabic translations; Aquinas himself was ignorant of Greek) as could be "reconciled" with Catholic doctrine by a judicious

[1] *Cf.* Part I, ch. 3.

" interpretation ". The Greek philosopher whose work was most extensively used was Aristotle; whom one would have imagined at first sight to be a most incongruous contributor to Christian truth.

By means of this synthesis, as expounded in innumerable volumes by St Thomas and his colleagues, a " reconciliation " was supposed to have been affected between Christian truth and Greek, or rather Arab, science, which would reclaim the educated world for Christianity in an age when its supersession was threatened by the scientific pantheism of the Arabs. It is obvious that the hope of reconciliation between Greek science, which owed its greatness precisely to its freedom from sacerdotal domination, and Catholic doctrine, the most intolerant and authoritarian system of ecclesiastical thought that the world has ever known, can never have been more than illusory; and, in fact, the Church had always to keep the Inquisition in reserve to quieten those who asked awkward questions about the alliance. Aristotle, who denied or doubted the existence of a personal God, was a somewhat curious ally for the Catholic whose doctrine taught the damnation of unbelievers! It is, in any case, obvious that a " philosophy " whose leading exponent declared that heretics should not be argued with, but incontinently put to death, a " science " that proscribed damnation for any solution of the eternal riddle except one decided by authority in advance, is, when judged by rational standards, neither genuine philosophy nor genuine science.

Scholastic " philosophy ", in spite of the great intellectual ability undoubtedly displayed by its chief exponents, belongs to the history, not of human philosophy, but of sacerdotal theocracy. It represented the form in which a pre-rational system sought to reconcile itself to a semi-civilized age by imparting an appearance of reason to conclusions in reality determined in advance by faith.

To-day the scholastic philosophy confronts the modern world as a survival of a bygone age, of a vanished era when the Temple was the centre of knowledge as well as of faith; the huge tomes of the "Angelic Doctor" taking their place in historic succession with, and in the same order of human thought as, those equally vast and imposing heaps of papyri stored up in the temple vaults of Karnak and Luxor, which contain the scholastic traditions of the priests of Ancient Egypt in the morning of the world, when priestly Pharaohs, themselves semi-divine, decided the affairs of earth by recourse to a hidden revelation whose sources lay altogether beyond human comprehension and whose mystic wisdom could be reverently interpreted by human knowledge only under sacerdotal auspices.

To judge of the impassable gulf which divides the Thomist philosophy from the world conception of the twentieth century, we have only to glance at its relation to evolution, the central and basic concept that is the core of contemporary philosophy. For it is not open to doubt that every mental advance of the past century has been bound up with this concept, and modern politics and economics are as much dependent on it as are modern anthropology and modern biology.

In particular Socialism, the chief present-day antagonist of the Papacy, is inseparably bound up with the idea of evolution, and would be inconceivable without it ; the Kantian law of ascending evolutionary stages in human history, each preparing the way for, and thus shortening the labours of, the succeeding stage, is an absolutely integral part of any philosophy of history which can claim to be at once socialistic and scientific, and has been accepted as such by all the classical masters of socialist philosophy.

Indeed, it would be as just and accurate to call Karl Marx " the Darwin of social science ", as to style Darwin " the Marx of natural history ". As Anton Pannekoek has clearly demonstrated, the work of these two great masters is complementary in its effects upon the evolution of human knowledge. *The Communist Manifesto* did for the evolution of human society what the *Descent of Man* did for the evolution of the human organism ; it raised it from the mists of mythology to the firm ground of science.

The crisis of the twentieth century is a crisis induced by evolution. It is a crisis pre-eminently of social science, of scientific socialism—and he who says science or socialism by that very fact affirms his belief in evolution, in the ever-realized potentiality of present human existence and of future human development.[1]

What is the relationship between Evolution, the living heart of modern science and modern philosophy, and the Church philosophy of the

[1] See F. Muéller-Lyer, *Phases of Social Development*, and **Anton Pannekoek**, *Marxism and Darwinism*.

Middle Ages which the Papacy seeks to rivet upon
the modern world, and which, should it survive
the present crisis, it will seek to impose upon
future ages? There is no ambiguity about its
attitude; the gulf between Rome and the modern
world is as absolute and impassable in the kingdom
of the intellect as in the spheres of politics and
ethics. In a world whose life-blood is change, the
Thomist Canute bids a peremptory halt to the
headlong advance of mankind. To the ceaseless
evolutionary transformation of species in the
natural world, to the endless variation of social
experiments and systems in the world of human
relations, the scholastic doctrine turns a blind and
uncomprehending eye. To the evolution of species
it still continues to oppose the everlastingly fixed
species of mediæval science, eternally separate,
for ever distinct from each other in their essential
" substance "; to the rise and fall of social systems,
still visible in the surviving settlements of prehistoric man, it opposes the " eternal " institutions of private property, social classes, and the
monogamous family. In a world in which the
stone age still lingers on, it blandly asserts that
the stone age and its patriarchal institutions never
existed, merely because St Thomas Aquinas had
never heard of them. Transferring the rigid
metaphysical conceptions of mediæval theology
into the dialectical world of ever-moving matter
and ever-changing appearance, it seeks to stabilize
for ever, *sub specie aeternitatis*, the limited world and
fixed institutions of mediæval times.

This static character was extended by the Thomist
philosophy to the Deity himself. The conception

of an evolutionary God, of a Deity who himself evolves along with the universe that he continually remakes anew, that Hegelian conception of an unfolding Idea immanent in the universe which permeates all distinctively modern religious thought, is utterly foreign to scholasticism, which, following Aristotle, defines God as " pure act ", *i.e.*, a Being in whom everything is already realized, and in whom, accordingly, no potentialities of future evolution can possibly exist. This Aristotelian conception of an immovable first cause, " the unmoved mover ", fitted admirably into the closed universe and static society of ancient and mediæval times, but is strangely out of harmony with the ever-changing universe and the ever-evolving society of our days. Modern evolution is totally irreconcilable with such a static conception.

In reality, the foundations of the Church philosophy are to be found, not in abstract doctrine, but in concrete history. As the author has elsewhere observed in this connection :

" The Thomist Aristotle was the philosopher of a stationary world in which time moved slowly, and society adhered to an immemorial conservatism undisturbed by technical change.

" Throughout its brilliant but unequal evolution, the culture of classical Greece was torn between the vast aspirations which its splendid intellect conjured up, and the severe inhibitions which were imposed upon it by its economic immaturity. The sharpest point in this perennial disequilibrium was expressed in the Attic tragedy, dominated by a brooding fate, the highest point which the literary art of the classical culture attained.

" As a brilliant living scholar has forcibly written in this connection : ' Fate is the limitation of technical means. It is the voice of blood, of sickness, of death, of all that limits man and prevents him from becoming " arrogant ".'[1]

" In the theological domain this attitude expressed itself in the definition of God as ' pure Act', beyond potentiality of any kind, *i.e.* a static God to whom the process of dialectical evolution is absolutely meaningless. This definition is that of Roman Catholic philosophy and theology to-day, which have adopted it officially. It is the basis of Catholic philosophy.

" To the historically informed Marxist there is no kind of mystery about this definition. It is the ideological expression of an immemorially stagnant Mediterranean world, wherein rapid change was unknown, where an unbroken tradition stretched back, uninterruptedly, to its unknown beginnings, where society, the ' Pure Act ', rested so firmly on a basis of slavery and of class rule, that it had no potentialities whatsoever of change. A society serenely aloof since its ' Primal Urge ', and able to remain calmly ' apathetic '—as Aristotle described the Deity— without thought of change. A society which throughout its vast antiquity maintained an even balance, unruffled by the impetus of technical progress. The Middle Ages, the ' classical ' epoch of Catholic philosophy, continued these conditions, accentuated them by the imposition

[1] L. D. Trotsky, *Literature and Revolution.*

of the dead hand of theological tradition, and modelled the eternal world upon the mediæval world with which, alone, it was acquainted here below."[1]

Such is, in effect, with but unavoidable modifications, the world which Catholicism to-day seeks to restore. It is a closed world, closed in thought, in technique, in social philosophy. It is a world utterly inconsistent with the actual state of present-day social and scientific knowledge; still less is it compatible with the vast potentialities held out by the process of modern evolution in every sphere.

A mediæval conception of civilization which negates the very idea of " progress ", a mediæval philosophy which denies all potentialities of change, represent a grotesquely incongruous spectacle in the twentieth century, when the scientific and industrial revolution of modern times is at last beginning to move forward with a speed, and towards a goal, that would have seemed utterly chimerical to all earlier ages, and, very especially, to the self-styled " age of faith ".

A metaphysic of " Pure Act " can never fit into a society of pure potentiality, as is the society of to-day. The declaration of the " Syllabus " of 1864, " Let him be anathema who affirms that the Roman Pontiff can reconcile himself with Liberalism, Progress, and modern civilization ", is now truer than ever. The mediæval and modern worlds cannot long co-exist in this headlong age of technical innovation as the essential soul and driving

[1] F. A. Ridley, *Marx, Aristotle, and the Black International*, " The New Adelphi ", January, 1933.

force of change. Rome is now threatened as she has never been threatened before; the forces opposed to her are incomparably stronger; the forces making for revolutionary change in all departments of life are immeasurably more potent, than were those which confronted her in the preceding crises of her history.

Rome has now, at last, come to the cross roads of destiny. The infallible Church must realize that modern civilization, if it continues, will infallibly destroy her. She can only hope to live amidst its ruins. A church whose declared motto is " For ever the same " cannot hope to survive for long in a world that is never the same !

The destruction of modern civilization has, therefore, become a *sine qua non* if Rome is to survive the crisis that at present confronts her. As the Papacy has clearly realized, the victory of socialism means the end of the Catholic world and of the Catholic Church. Hence the fanatical and morbid fear of a militant socialism that characterizes her utterances at the present time.

However, Socialism, her most immediate enemy, is itself far from being *sui generis*; it did not come fully grown into the world like a modern Pallas Athene. Socialism is the legitimate child of liberalism, and the " world revolution " has the French Revolution as its ancestor in direct line. Nor can Liberalism itself be considered in a manner consonant with history, unless it is regarded as the lineal offspring and heir of the Protestant Reformation, of the great religious revolution of the sixteenth century, from which the entire modern epoch derives; and it is well known that the

Reformation itself was but the successful culmination—operating under conditions more favourable to religious revolution than did its mediæval precursors—of the repeated attempts of nameless reformers of mediæval times to break off the yoke of Rome.

Hence the socialist crisis of our century, which now threatens the Papacy with final and irremediable ruin, represents the sum and culmination of that series of religious, intellectual, and political revolutions against the Papacy and against the dead hand of the mediæval Church, whose collective totality makes up the revolution of modern civilization against the yoke of pre-modern dogma. In fact, if Rome to-day faces the twin dragons of socialism and secularism, it was Luther and Calvin who first hatched the eggs, the Jacobin Club that reared them to maturity, and Marx and Lenin who taught them to fly ! And, as we have already seen, the Papacy fully comprehends this historic affiliation.

Hence the urgent task that contemporary history imposes upon the Papacy as the first law of its own continued existence and self-preservation is the destruction, not merely of socialism, its immediate enemy, but of the whole order of modern civilization, that incarnate revolt of reason against authority, and of humanism against revelation. Not merely is it necessary for Rome to snap the last link in the chain, socialism, but, to obliterate the whole co-ordinated series of cause and effect which dates back to the reformers in the field of religion, to Descartes in the realm of philosophy, to Galileo in the kingdom of science. The revolt of reason has now proceeded so far, and threatens such dire results to Rome, that she can only survive by destroying, not merely socialism, but the whole inheritance of modern civilization, whose final advance to political and economic rationalism, i.e. to socialism, means her final and irrevocable extinction.

For this achievement, however, the forces at the disposal of the contemporary Papacy are clearly insufficient. In an age dominated so extensively by science, an age in which, as Lecky happily observed, " The lightning-conductor, invented by the sceptic Franklin, defends our churches against the stroke of heaven ",[1]   the ecclesiastical army alone can no more overthrow Soviet Russia, win back defaulting Spain and Mexico, and check the advance of socialism and rationalism throughout the western world, than could the Papacy in the time of Hildebrand overthrow the powerful and civilized Arabs by means of its own unaided resources. To-day, as then, she seeks, and must find, allies. As in the eleventh century she found the Normans, whose religious zeal was coupled with an overmastering desire to destroy and plunder the wealthy Moslem civilization of the Near East, the chief enemy of the contemporary Papacy, so to-day she seeks twentieth-century Normans, whose hatred of socialism is coupled with an equal necessity for the subordination of all forms of rationalism to the blind yoke of an authoritarian régime. If such allies can be found, the way is open for a new era of Crusades, a new epoch of religious wars, an epoch in which the

[1] W. E. H. Lecky, *History of European Morals.*

Papacy and its temporal ally will hurl their combined forces against the world of modern civilization.

The ally is there ! For it so happens that the very speed and violence of change in the modern epoch has itself evoked a reaction of corresponding violence ; and, at the same pace that the social revolution advances, advances the Fascist reaction also. Moreover, history has imposed upon the contemporary political reaction tasks of a character broadly equivalent to the tasks imposed in our century upon the religious reaction itself.

For Fascism is a species of political " Catholicism ", as Catholicism itself is, in its attitude *vis à vis* modern culture, a kind of ecclesiastical " Fascism ". History imposes upon both these forms of reaction, the old and the new, the task of destroying utterly and irrevocably both socialism, the immediate enemy of both, and also the entire principle of modern rationalist civilization, whose final term and logical conclusion is represented by the social movements of the twentieth century. Hence, Fascism and Romanism, the two " Black Internationals ", represent a common bar to progress and a common need for its destruction, for the entire obliteration of the modern epoch, the era *par excellence* of the " revolt of reason ", of the progressive advance of mankind from the mists of superstition into the clear light of science.

To revert therefore to the historical parallel already suggested, the Fascists are the Normans of the twentieth century, and the era of the Crusades against the enemies of the church is already in being through their instrumentality and aid. Fascism and the Roman Catholic Church are the two principal forces opposed to the advance of European civilization at the present day, their enemies are the same, their needs are the same; their ideals and world philosophy do not essentially differ. An alliance with Fascism thus presents itself as the way out, as the effective solution, of the new crisis that threatens both alike with destruction. The Papacy now turns to the Fascists, to Hitler and Mussolini, as in mediæval times it turned to the Normans, Robert Guiscard and Godfrey de Bouillon. It is, accordingly, to this new " Holy Alliance ", to this new concordance between Rome and the secular reaction, that the third, remaining part of the present investigation is, accordingly, devoted.

END OF PART TWO

Note T : Liberalism and Socialism

The statement that Socialism derives from Liberalism is to be understood in a general and not in a particular sense. While Socialism, economic and cultural democracy, is the authentic heir and successor of Liberalism, political and social democracy, it does not necessarily follow that the same is true in every respect of every manifestation of Socialism. Thus, in contemporary Russia, where the Bolshevik régime took over a pre-liberal atmosphere, and had to govern a country still in the grip of illiteracy and priestcraft, many pre-liberal habits and institutions still survive: such as the retention of terrorism as a permanent institution of state, the quasi-religious veneration paid to the tomb of Lenin, the exaggerated regard for the *obiter dicta* of Stalin and his circle which at times gives to Bolshevism the appearance of a kind of " red Catholicism " ; all these and similar phenomena will necessarily disappear progressively as Russia approximates to genuine Socialism ; which, wherever it is able to develop naturally, represents the completion and consummation, of liberalism, and of its intellectual counterpart, rationalism.

Note U : The Papal Encyclicals on Socialism, and Infallibility

According to the definition of Papal Infallibility promulgated at the Vatican Council on July 18, 1870, the Pope is infallible only when he speaks in virtue of his office and defines a point of faith and morals as the ruler and representative of the Universal Church. This definition necessarily excludes the majority of Papal Encyclicals and pronouncements. It would seem, however, that the two Encyclicals which condemn socialism are, on Catholic principles, certainly infallible, and therefore irrevocable. Both Leo XIII and Pius XI spoke in their official capacities as rulers of the Universal Church, and, addressing the whole world, laid down the law on questions not merely of politics, but of morals also. It would therefore seem certain that the anti-socialist attitude proclaimed in both the Encyclicals, *Rerum Novarum* and *Quadragesimo Anno* is now an irrevocable part of Catholic dogma.

Note V: Encyclical of Leo XIII, "Aeterni Patris", August 4, 1879

" Now far above all other scholastic Doctors towers Thomas Aquinas, their master and prince. . . . Moreover, carefully distinguishing reason from faith, as is right, and yet joining them together in a harmony of friendship, he so guarded the rights of each, and so watched over the dignity of each, that, as far as man is concerned, reason can hardly now rise higher than she rose, borne up on the flight of Thomas ; and faith can hardly gain more and greater helps from reason than those which Thomas gave her."

The Encyclical officially installed Thomism as the standard philosophy of the church. A contemporary French Thomist, M. Jacques Maritain, has devoted a book, *Three Reformers*: *Luther, Descartes, Rousseau,* to proving that the revolt against scholasticism constitutes the starting-point of what is distinctive in modern thought.

Thomas Aquinas (1228-74) was an Italian of Norman descent, related to the Imperial house of Hohenstaufen. He was a Dominican, and author of numerous theological and philosophical works, of which the *Summa Theologica*, a compendium of Catholic doctrine, and the *Summa Contra Gentiles*, a summary of Catholic apologetics, are the chief. The modern scholastic revival is usually named after him. He is styled the " Angelic Doctor ".

PART THREE

THE HOLY ALLIANCE

The Papacy is the ghost of the Roman Empire sitting crowned in the grave thereof.—THOMAS HOBBES, *Leviathan* 1651.

Chapter I

THE RISE AND HISTORIC RÔLE OF FASCISM

Broadly speaking, we may say that every civilization hitherto known to mankind has passed successively through the stages of rise, maturity, and decay. Thus, in that earlier civilization of which we know most and which most resembles our own, the culture of classical antiquity, we can observe a period of ascension, a golden age of virile maturity, and a long dragging decay, which last endured so long and left so vivid an impression on mankind that "the decline of the Roman Empire" almost furnishes a descriptive title for an entire era of human history.

It has become evident in recent years that modern civilization, for all its quondam illusions of eternity, is repeating the same process. It, too, has known its epochs of rise and meridian, and is now experiencing its era of decay. In fact, just as the ancient civilization based economically on slave-capitalism knew in succession the stormy age of youth—preserved in the Homeric poems, the Golden Age of the "Glory that was Greece", and finally the epoch of the Cæsars, the "Fascist" era of the ancient world, so also modern civilization, based economically on wage labour, has experienced a similar succession.

During the four and a half centuries that separated

the discovery of the world market, which inaugurated modern capitalist civilization, from the present day, Europe has in turn witnessed the stormy era of revolutions which broke the yoke of mediævalism, the period of unparalleled expansion which marked the imperialist heyday of world capitalism in the nineteenth century, and finally, the present era of decline, whose supreme expression and embodiment is Fascism in the contemporary world.

In fact, looking at the question from the broad standpoint of universal history, and not from any narrow political platform, Fascism, and the Fascist movements which embody it in action, are the formula of the decay of modern capitalist civilization, just as the Roman Empire of the Cæsars represented the similarly conscious passage of the classical civilization from maturity to decay. Cæsarism, Fascism and the Totalitarian State all alike represent, indeed, the same social phenomenon. The historic task of the Cæsars of Imperial Rome, as I have defined elsewhere, was, at bottom, simply this : " They averted dissolution by stabilizing decay : " The same task is performed by the Fascist dictatorships of to-day.[1]

We may define Fascism, considered as a sociological phenomenon, as an artificial attempt to support an effete economic and social system by the aid of the crutches of dictatorship and repression, by means of a Totalitarian state which will artificially impede the natural evolution of society. In that ultimate historic sense, while the

---

[1] F. A. Ridley, *Julian the Apostate and the Rise of Christianity.* See Note W, pp. 172-3.

name "Fascist" is new, what it represents is as old as civilization; the artificial effort of a dying society to prolong its existence long after it has exhausted its social function and, consequently, its natural right to live. As such, it is everywhere characterized by refusal to face the possibility of future evolution and by a hankering after an idealized past.

In this respect, all the historic forms of Fascism concur. Augustus, the founder of the Fascist Empire of the Cæsars, bade Vergil, his court poet, devote the *Aeneid*, his *magnum opus*, to the celebration of the golden age of the distant past; Ignatius Loyola, the master of mediæval Fascism—as Jesuitism was styled above—laid down as an iron law: "No novelties in theology"; respect the authority of the past. While the Fascist dictators of to-day, Mussolini, Hitler, and Franco, as is well known, never tire of calling attention to the glories of the Rome of the Cæsars, the Germany of the *Niebelungenlied*, and the Spain of Columbus. Atavism is, in fact, so far from being accidental to this creed, that it is found at all times, in every Fascist state. That this is so, indicates the essentially reactionary and retrogressive nature of this social phenomenon.

The period immediately following the world war of 1914-18 was marked pre-eminently by the rise of Fascism. From Mussolini's "March on Rome" in October, 1922 down to the March on Madrid being conducted by General Franco at the time these lines are written, the past decade and a half has been signalized by a whole series of Fascist coups, both in Europe and in other parts of the world that model themselves upon European institutions.

As a result, not merely do Fascist or semi-Fascist states exist in Germany, Italy, Austria, Portugal, Japan, Paraguay, etc., but aggressive Fascist movements have arisen all over the world, and particularly in Europe, the Fascist continent of origin, which at present threaten with destruction both the institutions that derive from the recent past and the movements that aspire to the immediate future : the Fascist state making no distinction between liberalism, the classic philosophy of the nineteenth century, and socialism, the classic philosophy of the twentieth, but involving both impartially in a common ruin.

In fact, what the Holy Alliance—the union of reactionary conservatism—was to the early nineteenth century, the Fascist " International "—as it may be somewhat loosely styled—is for the world of the early twentieth. The part played in European politics by Metternich and Nicholas I of Russia in the generation after the world war of the last century, as the arch-priests of reaction in the generation between 1814-48, is now paralleled by that of Hitler and Mussolini. Fascism and Catholicism constitute the " Holy Alliance " of this century. They represent, as we shall see, the classical form of reaction that our age has so far evolved.

When considered in its international aspect as a social and cultural, or rather anti-cultural movement, the general historic rôle of Fascism is plainly evident and may be briefly defined. Its immediate aim is to save vested interests, and in particular the formerly useful but now historically obsolete institution of private property, involving human servitude, from the advance of economic democracy—*i.e.*, socialism. That this is so can be proved from the undoubted fact that wherever a Fascist movement has arisen, it has done so in answer to the threat of social revolution, and has postured before the world as a professed anti-socialist movement.

None the less, Fascism, as a logical form of the twentieth-century reaction, while primarily an anti-socialist movement, is far from exhausting its historic function by assuming that rôle ; it is also necessary for it to close all the highways both in thought and action that lead, or are capable of leading, to socialism. A glance at the historic circumstances that condition both progress and reaction in this century suffices to demonstrate that this must be so.

As already observed, socialism is not an historical "sport". It does not just grow, like Topsy in the nursery story. On the contrary, we must recall its genealogy. Socialism descends from Liberalism, which in its turn descends from the Reformation. In order to destroy Socialism, therefore, as a political and economic, as well as a cultural and historic force, it is equally necessary to destroy Liberalism and to repudiate the Reformation.

The Fascist leaders have proved capable of making this deduction. It is well known that in a Fascist state Liberalism and Rationalism, and, where it asserts its original principle, even Protestantism itself, have fallen under the ban as completely and effectively as any form of Communism, Socialism or Anarchism. Liberalism and Freemasonry, the political and anti-clerical progressive forces, are *per se* illegal in every Fascist State, while in contemporary Germany these Protestant theologians, such as Karl Barth, who retain the uncompromising spirit of early Protestantism, are either imprisoned in concentration camps, or else driven into exile.

Fascism itself, no less than the Papacy, recognizes the family tree of modern thought and progress, and is resolved to cut it down, beginning with its roots that plunge far back into history. Fascism, in short, develops social reaction to the same logical conclusion as does Roman Catholicism in the case of religious reaction. In its war against socialism it does not confine its task of destruction to that political creed, but extends it to the whole order of thought and practice of which Socialism is the final term. Fascism aims at the overthrow of the whole order of modern rationalism. Its goal is the destruction of modern thought in its entirety, nor can it otherwise fulfil its historic mission of safeguarding absolute privilege. A glance at its characteristic doctrines will be sufficient to demonstrate that this is the case, and that nothing other or less than the complete and irrevocable destruction of the entire rationalist civilization of modern times is its conscious and avowed aim.

Note W : *Cæsarism and Fascism*

The dictatorship of the Cæsars arose at the end of the period of acute social disintegration that marked the last years of the Roman Republic.

Beginning as a demagogic movement of the lower middle class (*equites*), the régime of the Cæsars ended by evolving a Totalitarian state which ruthlessly suppressed both social disorder and individual volition. By means of a policy of extreme authoritarianism, every kind of social disintegration was stopped, and ancient society was thus artificially prolonged long after the system of slave-economics had ceased to be a socially progressive force. The social rôle of Cæsarism was thus broadly identical with that which Fascism seeks to play in the conditions of the twentieth century; the forcible stabilization of outworn forms of society by means of a Totalitarian state, which itself culminated in a permanent dictatorship. The admiration so often expressed by Mussolini, the founder of modern Fascism, for his classical prototype, Julius Cæsar, and his selection of the name and emblem of his movement from the authoritarian symbols of ancient Rome, is, consequently, a good deal more than an individual whim. It has a social and historic, as well as a personal, significance.[1]

---

[1] " Fascism " is translated from the Italian word " Fascismo " —*i.e.* the " binding together " of the Lictors' rods, the symbol of authority carried before the magistrates of ancient Rome.

CHAPTER II

THE DOCTRINES OF FASCISM

FASCISM, unlike Catholicism, has nothing that resembles a formal system of canonical dogma. Nevertheless, there is a group of leading ideas sufficiently definite to be made the subject of analysis which may be said to be inseparable from Fascism. The following sketch of these Fascist tenets is taken in the main from the article on "Fascism" in the 14th volume of the *Enciclopedia Italiana* (1932). This article, written by Mussolini himself, is the nearest approach to a planned exposition of Fascism as a system of codified doctrine that has so far appeared, and, in view of its author's unique position in the Fascist world, may be taken as an authoritative definition.

The article is translated under the title of *The Political and Social Doctrine of Fascism*. Unless otherwise stated, all quotations in the ensuing chapter are from this pamphlet.

The Fascist creed presents the initial paradox that it is at once international and intensely nationalistic: international in the sense that it exists to defend reactionary interests on an international scale, nationalistic in that "sacred egoism" is an invariable characteristic of every Fascist state. While differing in certain local matters, Fascism,

174

wherever it exists, will be found to present the following characteristics.[1]

1. Fascism is essentially an authoritarian system, anti-socialist, anti-democratic, and anti-libertarian. On this aspect of Fascism Mussolini writes as follows :

" The foundation of Fascism is the conception of the State, its character, its duty, and its aim. Fascism conceives of the state as an absolute, in comparison with which all individuals or groups are relative, only to be conceived of in their relation to the state. . . .

" When the conception of the state declines, and disunifying and centrifugal tendencies prevail, whether of individuals or of particular groups, the nations where such phenomena appear are on their decline . . . Such a conception of life makes Fascism the complete opposite of that doctrine, the base of so-called scientific and Marxian Socialism, the materialist conception of history, according to which the history of human civilization can be explained simply through the conflict of interest among the various social groups and by the change and development in the means and instruments of production . . . .

" And if the economic conception of history is denied, according to which theory men are no more than puppets, carried to and fro by the waves of chance, while the real directing forces are quite out of their control, it follows that the existence of an unchangeable and unchanging class war is also denied, the natural progeny of the economic conception of history. And above all Fascism

[1] See Note X, p. 182.

denies that class war can be the preponderant force in the transformation of society. These two fundamental concepts of socialism being thus refuted, nothing is left of it but the sentimental aspiration—as old as humanity itself—towards a social convention in which the sorrows and sufferings of the humblest shall be alleviated. But here again Fascism repudiates the conception of " economic " happiness to be realized by Socialism and, as it were, at a given moment in economic evolution to assure to everyone the maximum of well-being . . . .

" After socialism, Fascism combats the whole complex system of democratic ideology, and repudiates it, whether in its theoretical or in its practical application. Fascism denies that the majority, by the simple fact that it is a majority, can direct human society. It denies that numbers alone can govern by means of a periodical consultation, and it affirms the immutable, beneficial and fruitful inequality of mankind, which can never be permanently levelled through the mere operation of a mechanical process such as universal suffrage. . . .

" . . . Fascism denies in democracy the absurd, conventional untruth of political equality dressed out in the garb of collective irresponsibility, and the myth of happiness and indefinite progress."

2. Fascism is imperialistic and militaristic. The following sentences of Mussolini have since found a practical confirmation in the conquest of Ethiopia : " Above all, Fascism, the more it considers and observes the future and the development of humanity, quite apart from political conceptions

of the moment, believes neither in the possibility, nor in the utility, of perpetual peace. It thus repudiates the doctrine of pacifism—born of a renunciation of the struggle and an act of cowardice in the face of sacrifice. War alone brings up to its highest tension all human energy and puts the stamp of nobility upon the peoples who have the courage to meet it. All other trials are substitutes, which never really put men in the position where they have to make the great decision—the alternative of life or death. Thus a doctrine which is founded upon this harmful postulate of peace is hostile to Fascism. For Fascism, the growth of Empire, that is to say the expansion of the nation, is an essential manifestation of vitality and its opposite a sign of decadence. Peoples which are rising, or rising again after a period of decadence, are always imperialist; any renunciation is a sign of decay and of death.

" This anti-pacifist spirit is carried by Fascism even into the life of the individual. . . .

" It is the education to combat, the acceptation of the risks which combat implies, and a new way of life for Italy.

" Fascism repudiates any universal embrace."

Thus Mussolini, the first person in the Fascist Godhead, on the subject of authoritarianism and militarism. His German co-divinity, the second person, may also be cited on these topics :

" Democracy in the West is the forerunner of Marxism, which would be inconceivable without Democracy. The most sacred right of our nation is to cultivate with the German plough land won by the German sword." [1]

[1] A. Hitler, *My Struggle*.

3. Fascism is, essentially, an anti-rationalist philosophy, it believes in action, not in theory, it exalts will against reason, as the dominant characteristic of human life. Thus Mussolini : " Fascism uses in its construction whatever elements in the liberal, social or democratic doctrines still have a living value, it maintains all the certainties which we owe to history, but it rejects all the rest —that is to say, the conception that there can be any doctrine of unquestioned efficacy for all times and all peoples. . . .

" . . . Every doctrine tends to direct human activity towards a determined objective, but the action of men also reacts upon the doctrine, transforms it, adapts it to new needs, or supersedes it with something else. A doctrine then must be no mere exercise in words, but a living act, and thus the value of Fascism lies in the fact that it is veined with pragmatism, but at the same time has a will to exist and a will to power, a firm front in face of the reality of ' violence '.

" . . . The Fascist state is an embodied will to power and government. The Roman ideal is here an ideal of force in action."

Sir Oswald Mosley, Mussolini's British disciple and would-be imitator, endorses this conception of Fascism. " Fascism is, above all, a doctrine of action." While it is well known that in the German conception of Fascism " blood " and " race " (the " Aryans ") play an all-important part.

4. Fascism is favourable to religion *and particularly to Roman Catholicism as the most authoritarian expression* of religion.

On this point both Mussolini and Hitler, the

arch-priests of European Fascism, can be cited without ambiguity. Mussolini writes :

" The Fascist state is not indifferent to the fact of religion in general, or to that particular and positive faith which is Italian Catholicism. The state professes no theology, but a morality, and in the Fascist state religion is considered as one of the deepest manifestations of the spirit of man ; thus it is not only respected, but defended and protected. The Fascist state has never tried to create its own God, as at one moment Robespierre and the wildest extremists of the Convention tried to do ; nor does it vainly seek to obliterate religion from the hearts of men, as does Bolshevism. Fascism respects the God of the ascetics, the saints and heroes, and equally God as He is perceived and worshipped by simple people."

Adolf Hitler, in his autobiography *My Struggle*, thus refers to Catholicism in particular : " Much may be learned from the Roman Catholic Church. Though the body of its doctrine clashes with exact science and research on many points—unnecessarily in certain respects—the Church is not prepared to sacrifice a single syllable of its doctrines. It has realized very correctly that its power of resistance depends not on being more or less in harmony with the scientific events of the moment —which are, as a matter of fact, always altering— but rather in clinging firmly to dogmas once laid down, which, on the whole, do express the character of the Faith. As a consequence the Church stands firmer than ever before." [1]

---

[1] A. Hitler, *My Struggle*, p. 184 of abridged English translation.

That the authoritarian principle in Fascism sympathizes with the similar principle of Catholicism may be inferred from the following observation of Hitler :

" There are many signs of a struggle, every day increasing in violence, against the dogmatic principles of the various churches, without which, in practice, religious belief is inconceivable in this world of humanity. The general mass of a nation do not consist of philosophers, faith for them is very largely the sole basis for a moral view of life. . . . If religious doctrine and faith really get a grip on the mass of the people, the absolute authority of that faith is then the whole basis of its efficacy. What then ordinary custom is for the general life, the law is for the state and dogma is for ordinary religion. . . . The attack upon dogma is in itself, therefore, very like the struggle against the general legal principles of the state, and just as the latter would end in complete state anarchy, the former would end in hopeless religious nihilism " [1]

5. Fascism may be considered, from certain points of view at least, as a revolt of the countryside against the town. The original Fascist bands of Hitler and Mussolini were recruited largely from peasants, and both the present German and Italian governments make the perpetuation of a strong peasantry into a political objective, and direct legislation, accordingly, towards this end. In German Fascist philosophy " blood and soil " represent the highest object of attainment at which

[1] Hitler, *op. cit.*, pp. 114-5.

a virile nation should aim. The German philosopher, Oswald Spengler, indeed, defines the " decadent bourgeois culture " which Fascism overthrows as a " Megalopolitan " culture (i.e. a culture dominated by overgrown cities) against which Fascism represents the uprising of the virile rural elements.[1]

Such are the principal features of present-day Fascism considered as an international movement of contemporary reaction. In spite of the demagogic character which is an invariable accompaniment of Fascism in all places where it makes its appearance, the features outlined above represent, beyond a doubt, its genuine nature as a movement in action. And this is the more important, since like such earlier forms of reaction as Cæsarism, Jesuitism, and the Holy Alliance, the theory of Fascism followed, and did not precede, its action ; the ideas of Fascism merely sum up its practice retrospectively. " In the beginning was the act " may, in fact, be styled the motto of international Fascism ; like all movements which arise, not from ideas, but from vested interests already in existence, the theory of Fascism reflects accurately its observed practice. Like Catholicism, but unlike Rationalism, its thought follows upon and does not anticipate its action.[2]

Thus, then, the European reaction of the twentieth century appears before the world as a system, authoritarian in politics, anti-rational and pragmatic in thought, sympathetic to tradition in the moral and religious fields, with a strong bias

[1] O. Spengler, *The Hour of Decision*.
[2] See Note Y, p. 183.

towards authoritarianism in the religious domain. Authoritarian, traditional, professedly irrational in its world philosophy, scoffing at progress, suppressing individualism, extolling the herd, insisting on a military obedience, demanding a blind submission, such is Fascism, the form taken by the political reaction of our generation. It remains to consider the relations of this system with the system of Roman Catholicism, the leading protagonist of the contemporary religious reaction, as, under the Papal dictatorship, it girds up its loins to do battle with the crisis of the twentieth century.

Note X : *Fascism and Anti-Semitism*

The chief difference between German and Italian Fascism is that the former, but not the latter, is anti-semitic. Anti-semitism, however, while congruous with the nationalistic spirit of Fascism, is not absolutely essential to it. In Germany there were both local economic reasons and ancient traditions, dating back to mediæval times, that favoured anti-semitism, which existed long before the advent of Hitler to power. In Italy these motives were lacking, and several members of the dictator's entourage are of Jewish origin, including his official biographer, Margherita Sarfatti. While nationalism is an integral and indispensable part of Fascism everywhere, racialism—*i.e.* persecuting nationalism—is an optional adjunct to the régime, and its appearance or non-appearance would appear to depend entirely on local conditions.

Note Y : *Fascism and Demagogy*

Ever since the mid-nineteenth century, when the necessities of expanding capitalism compelled the introduction of working-class popular education, reaction has been compelled to assume demagogic forms in order to deceive the multitude into a belief that it is really acting in their interests. Disræli, the inventor of " Tory Democracy ", was the real pioneer of this alliance of conservatism and demagogy, and may thus be said to be the stepfather, at least, of Fascism. All the contemporary Fascist dictators are expert demagogues. Hitler, in his autobiography, lays down elaborate rules for the conduct of the technique of mass deception. The official title of his party—the " National Socialist Workers' Party "—is itself part of the deception. Mussolini defines the era of Fascism as " a century of the Left ".[1] Similarly the French Fascist historian, Auguste Bailly, defines Fascism as " a dictatorship of the Left ", and contrasts it, as such, with earlier dictatorships of the Right, such as that of his subject, Cardinal Richelieu.[2]

Actually, of course, we must judge Fascism by its deeds and not its words, and these are so purely atavistic and reactionary as to stamp it as a movement of the most retrograde character imaginable. That it is obliged to cloak its actions in a demagogic fashion is a consequence of the times we live in, and not of the movement itself. Its genuine character

[1] Mussolini, *ut supra.*
[2] A. Bailly, *Richelieu the Cardinal Dictator*, p. 134.

is that indicated in the text. This in no way excludes the undeniable fact that Fascism exacts a heavy price from the reactionary interests, in whose service it works. As we have already seen, the same was also true of Jesuitism, the ecclesiastical Fascism of the epoch of the Counter-Reformation.[1]

[1] *Cf.* Part I, ch. 4.

Chapter III

FASCISM AND ROMAN CATHOLICISM

It is evident to any unbiased observer that Fascism and the Roman Catholic Church, the two " black Internationals ", as we may call them, are the two chief forces making for reaction in the contemporary Western world, and the two chief obstacles to the solution of the crisis of the twentieth century along the lines of social and scientific progress. These two movements, which alike arose in Rome, are the dams built up against the incoming tide of modern progress. Once they were out of the way, that tide could and would rush on at the great speed the hitherto unthought-of potentialities of our times now permit, and no man can say to what heights the human race could not in that event attain, in view of the illimitable forces which the Machine Age has unloosed, and whose immeasurable resources are now at the disposal of mankind for the first time in its history. In the meantime, what are the relations between these two principal forms of the present-day reaction, between the political Cæsarism of Fascism and the ecclesiastical Cæsarism of Papal Rome ?

After the foregoing examination of them both, we need not spend much time on such an inquiry ; it is evident that the two great reactionary movements of contemporary life have a great many points of contact. Below, we enumerate the leading ideas that they have in common.

1. Fascism and Catholicism are both anti-socialist, anti-Communist and anti-Labour; for both the destruction of the parties of the Left is a *sine qua non* of their continued existence. Both alike can only solve the crisis of the twentieth century, the crisis pre-eminently of Socialism and of social evolution, by the destruction of Socialism and the consequent repudiation of economic democracy and the denial of economic and social justice.

2. Both alike are authoritarian, and therefore anti-rationalist. Their common need is the entire destruction of the secular civilization of modern times, founded upon autonomous human reason. Both alike oppose and, where possible, extirpate liberalism, democracy, free-thought and even Protestantism. Both alike are hostile, not merely to Socialism, but to the whole distinctive tradition of modern thought, whose logical culmination and completion socialism is, and without whose pre-existence the crisis of our century is inconceivable.

3. Both are atavistic in their relation to culture. Both deny progress in explicit terms (*cf.* Pius IX and Mussolini *ut supra*); both idealize the past. Both alike oppose the extension of modern knowledge to modern social life. Both condemn, for example, any and every form of eugenics and birth-control, the most important contribution made by the twentieth century to social welfare. Both demand the military virtue of blind obedience from their subjects.

4. Both exalt the country and the peasantry

against the town. Both exalt the countryside, the static element in human life, against the town, the progressive element which has created all human civilization. The economic ideal of both Fascism and the Papacy is a virile but obedient peasantry; both idealize what Marx has aptly termed " The idiocy of rural life "; both extol the unprogressive element in human society against the progressive.[1]

5. Both alike repudiate " sweet reasonableness " and conversion by persuasion; both are persecuting creeds. The mediæval Inquisition and the Counter-Reformation Index are matched and paralleled by the Fascist " Tribunal for the Defence of the State ", the Nazi concentration camps, and the *auto da fè*, constituted by the burning of books hostile to the régime or which for some other reason have incurred its ban. In contradiction to Liberalism, Fascism believes in imposing its beliefs by force, and Terrorism of a permanent character, systematically organized upon principles identical with those of the Inquisition, forms a regular constituent of every Fascist State. Fascism has refuted the prediction of Professor Bury that the mediæval era of persecution cannot recur.[2]

7. Both are " Totalitarian " States—neither is " agnostic " or indifferent to any sphere of its subjects' lives—both alike claim to exercise control over every department of human life and activity. Both recognize and practise the " unity of theory and practice " which characterizes every species

[1] *Cf.* Hitler, *My Struggle*, and the publications of the Catholic " Distributists ", e.g. Hilaire Belloc, *The Servile State*, etc.

[2] J. B. Bury, *History of Freedom of Thought*.

of Totalitarian State at all times.   Both watch
vigilantly over the thoughts, no less than over the
actions, of their subjects.   (" Agnosticism " is the
Fascist description of the political *laissez-faire* of
Liberalism.   In contemporary Italy it is a term of
abuse.)

8. Both rest on, and culminate in, permanent
dictatorships vested in an individual who embodies
Tradition and is consequently unerring, as the Pope
is infallible by virtue of the Vatican Decree.   One
of the ten points of the " Fascist Decalogue ",
to which every Fascist must give verbal assent—is
" Mussolini is always right ".   After the massacre
of June 30, 1934, Hitler declared that henceforth
he would do the thinking of the German nation
for it.   The " Leader " principle is an integral
part of both the Fascist and the Catholic systems,
of the former ever since it began, of the latter actually since Hildebrand (1072-85) the founder of the
Ultramontane Papacy, officially since July 18,
1870, the date of the Vatican Decree.

9. The common enemy of both systems is human
evolution and its interpreter, human thought.
The first effective law of both Catholicism and
Fascism is the " Law against dangerous thoughts ".
For Thought, whose province it is to dispel falsehood, will act as a deadly corrosive to both systems
which negate the truth of human existence in the
twentieth century.   Both systems must end evolution, or evolution will surely end them !   The alliance of the two reactionary systems, which we are
about to discuss, arises from this fundamental
fact.

.   .   .   .   .

It is evident from the above comparisons that Fascism and Catholicism are united by the two strongest forces which can unite either men or institutions, *viz.,* a common world outlook and common enemies. They have, it is true, some potential points of mutual hostility, but these are quite secondary when compared with the numerous points which we see them to possess in common. They fall into the background compared with the overmastering need for self-preservation which unites them in face of the advance of human reason and of the social forces which embody it, whose triumph spells the end of reaction alike in its political, economic and ecclesiastical forms ; moreover, the points of difference which separate the Papacy from Fascism are of such a character that *they can only operate on the morrow of victory.* Until the victory is won, they will remain dormant and inoperative. It will, however, be necessary to glance at them later.[1]

As a result, the road is now open for an effective alliance between the two chief forms of the contemporary reaction, Fascism and Catholicism, an alliance so congruous to both that it has come into existence in country after country by a kind of natural volition, and has been made known to the entire world by the events now occurring in Spain, where the war against socialism, rationalism, and democracy has now assumed the proportions of an international Crusade of both Fascism and Catholicism against the forces of progress. It is, therefore, both opportune and necessary to glance at this alliance, and, turning from theory

[1] See Pt. 3, ch. 5, " The Two Totalitarian States ".

to the practice which is its expression, to investigate the new Holy Alliance which over half Europe confronts the march of social evolution and to-day repeats in Spain the experiences, the horrors, and the fanaticism of the era of the mediæval Crusades.

Note Z : The Papal Encyclical " Divini Redemptoris ", March 18, 1937

On March 18, 1937, Pope Pius XI issued an encyclical in which, not content with condemning Communism as the foremost enemy of " Christian civilization ", he explicitly recommended the " guild system ", the economics of the " corporative " state of Fascism, as not merely the most effective antidote to Communism, but as essentially superior to the *laissez-faire* economics of liberalism, the " abuses " of which it corrects in the interests of the working classes. This encyclical constitutes a landmark in the relations of the Papacy with Fascism, since it is the first overt declaration of their already existing alliance. It was, doubtless, no accident that it appeared just at the point when the Spanish civil war began to take a turn prejudicial to the armies " of Christ " (*i.e.* Franco) and Mussolini. The Papacy has always refrained from showing its hand until forced by circumstances to abandon its cautious attitude and come out into the open.

Chapter IV

THE HOLY ALLIANCE

In this chapter we touch on the outstanding features of the Catholic-Fascist Alliance in each of the countries where it has successively appeared. No formal alliance has thus far been proclaimed between the " high contracting parties ", such as inaugurated " the Holy Alliance " between Russia, Austria and Prussia in 1815.[1] Rome has always been very cautious in her political commitments. It will be understood that in the space at the writer's disposal it is not possible to do more than indicate the leading features of this alliance in bare outline ; a separate volume would be required to trace the successive interactions of Papal-Fascist diplomacy in detail. As Fascism is primarily a nationalistic phenomenon, it will be convenient to trace the growth of the Fascist-Catholic alliance in the three major fields wherein it has so far appeared, Italy, Germany, and in particular Spain, where that alliance is most open and effective. Subsequently, a brief glance will be directed at the lesser Fascist and Catholic countries wherein are visible signs of an extension of the alliance. (The Preamble to the " Holy Alliance " was signed on Sept. 26, 1815, by the Tsar of Russia, the Emperor

[1] See Note AA, p. 198.

of Austria and the King of Prussia—the three great
reactionary European States of the time.
*It expressed political reaction in the terms
of religious mysticism.*)

(a) *THE PAPACY AND ITALIAN FASCISM*

As is well known, Mussolini, the founder of
Italian Fascism, was originally an atheist. In July,
1904 the future Dictator, then an anarchist of the
extreme Left, wrote a widely-circulated pamphlet
which popularized the views of Michael Bakunin,
who regarded " God and the State " as the chief
enemies of mankind and the chief obstacles to the
mental and political emancipation of humanity.[1]
Mussolini embraced Nationalistic views during
the World War, and founded the Fascist party immediately after it. Originally, Fascism claimed to
be a party of the Left ; the original programme of
the Party, published in March, 1919, demanded,
inter alia, the disestablishment and disendowment
of the Roman Catholic Church in Italy. After the
" March on Rome " which installed him in power,
Mussolini's policy at first brought him into hostile
relations with the Church. This was partly due to
the political opposition between the Fascists and
the " Populist " Party of the priest Don Sturzo,
subsequently exiled from Italy, and partly to the
" Totalitarian " activities of the Fascist State,
which endeavoured to suppress the youth organizations raised by the Catholic movement for " Social

[1] See Note AA, page 198.

Action ". This action led to acrimonious relations between the Papacy and Italian Fascism. The Pope, in his encyclical on " Catholic Action " in 1931, even went as far as to refer to " the pagan worship of the State " which characterized the Fascist régime.

The Papacy has, however, always known when it is or is not expedient to push matters to extremes. To-day it knows that its real enemy is not Fascism, but rather those forces which Fascism exists to destroy, Socialism, rationalism and the modern spirit. Compared with these, any danger represented by the excessive power of the Fascist State is altogether secondary. In the general scheme of things in the twentieth century, Fascism must present itself as a potential ally of the Papacy ; however much it may irritate the Church authorities by its " Totalitarian " claims, yet these are always secondary matters ; fundamentally both, the Papacy and Fascism, are on the same side of the fence in the struggle of the contemporary world. To-morrow—" Let to-morrow decide to-morrow's problems " has always been a maxim of Papal diplomacy. These considerations were not lost on the singularly able and ultra-reactionary Pius XI, who, prior to his election as Pope (Feb. 2, 1922) had been archbishop of Milan, then the head-quarters of the Fascist Movement in the days before it assumed power, and whose own elevation inside a year to the successive ranks of archbishop, Cardinal, and Pope, was primarily due to the prominent part he had played as Nuncio in Warsaw at the time of the Bolshevik invasion of Poland in August, 1920.

These considerations bore fruit on February 11, 1929, when the Lateran Treaty restored the peace between the Papacy and Italy which had been broken in September 1870, when the Italian army had occupied Rome and forcibly ended the Papal States. The Lateran Treaty released " the prisoner in the Vatican ", and added to the polity of Europe a new state—" The Vatican City "—the smallest State in Europe, about 110 acres, a little larger than St James' Park in area, but within that State the Pope is a reigning monarch. The Treaty of the Lateran, signed by Mussolini and by Cardinal Gasparri, at that time Papal Secretary of State, owes its historic importance however, not to the addition of a Lilliputian State to the political world, but to the fact that it settled the outstanding differences between the Papacy and Italian Fascism, the prototype of World Fascism. This is what constitutes the epoch-making significance of the Lateran Treaty, it left both parties free to contract a subsequent alliance in the political and cultural fields.

Under the terms of that Treaty, the Pope was recognized as the ruler of the Vatican State, and the Italian Government further agreed to pay the sum of $1\frac{3}{4}$ milliard (1750 million) Italian lire as compensation to the Papacy for the loss of the Papal States in 1870. The Pope, on his part, renounced his claim to the lost States, and thus " buried the hatchet " with Italy.

Since Feb. 11, 1929, the road has been open for a " united front " between the Vatican and the Fascist régime. In spite of some subsequent friction in 1931-2, the alliance has, on the whole, worked harmoniously, and Mussolini has justified his Papal sobriquet of " a man raised up by God ". An outward and visible sign of this metamorphosis of the quondam anarchist-atheist into the " man of God " was displayed to the world in 1932, when the ex-terrorist disciple of Bakunin walked to the tomb of St Peter, was sprinkled with holy water, and subsequently went to the altar and prayed—to what God?—over the sepulchre of the apostle, that eponymous martyr at the hands of Mussolini's admired prototypes, those excellent " Fascists ", the Cæsars of Imperial Rome. The subsequent relations of the two Romes have been in keeping with this excellent beginning.

The outstanding example of this friendly co-operation is afforded by the Italian conquest of Ethiopia in 1935-6. This imperialistic enterprise was openly favoured by the Papacy in spite of its wantonly aggressive character and flagrant barbarities against unarmed civilians, which shocked the conscience of the civilized world, including non-Catholic religious opinion. The Papacy publicly applauded the imperialistic desire for expansion of this " peaceful nation ", high Italian prelates transformed themselves into jingoistic recruiting-sergeants, and the final climax of the war, or, to speak more accurately, of the mass murder of unarmed primitives by modern science, the capture of Addis Ababa and the flight of the Negus, was celebrated at the Pope's order by thanksgiving services and the ringing of bells in all the churches of Italy. The Pope, in fact, was only repeating the historic thanksgiving that Gregory XIII (1572-85) had ordered to celebrate the famous massacre of the French Protestants on St Bartholomew's Eve, August 24, 1572—an event greeted in Rome with similar rejoicings. After all, is not the motto of the Papacy still " *semper eadem*—" For ever the same " ?

The existence of Ethiopia had always been an obstacle to the spread of Roman Catholicism in Africa. In the seventeenth century the Ethiopian Empire had expelled the Jesuit missionaries, and the native Coptic church had always resisted the blandishments of Rome. Consequently, this church of obstinate schismatics had always been unpopular with the Popes, and its overthrow was a matter of rejoicing to the Vatican. Had not a Roman expert already pronounced that the Ethiopian church was " considerably the most backward part of the entire Christian family ? " The fall of the Ethiopian Empire would prepare the way for the destruction of an autonomous schismatic and heretical church. As for such mundane considerations as truth, justice, international morality, the use of poison gas, and the wholesale maiming of unarmed civilians, what do these weigh against the eternal salvation of the souls of the benighted Ethiopians ? In any case, it is common ground among theologians that Providence " moves in mysterious ways its wonders to perform ". Even the Italian Air Force may prove a messenger from heaven ! [1]

And so, we find the alliance of the Papacy and Fascism in full operation in " Italian East Africa ". We have lately learnt that " to assist the process of

[1] See Rev. Dr. Adrian Fortescue, *The Lesser Eastern Churches*, p. 297.

reconstruction, plans for far-reaching collaboration between the Holy See and the Fascist state in Abyssinia are being studied. One generous gesture. The Vatican, which possesses the best-equipped polyglot printing sets in the world, has sent to Addis Ababa a complete font of Amharic type, together with an instructor. But for this there will be payment. As far as the concessions to the Church are known as yet, they envisage the exclusive use of Italian missionaries in that country and the establishment there of twelve apostolic vicarates and prefectures.[1] Papal and Fascist imperialism are working hand in glove in East Africa, a very dangerous policy for the future of Catholicism in that continent, and one against which Pope Benedict XV explicitly warned his successors in his Encyclical on Foreign Missions.[2]

At the present time, the Holy Alliance between the Rome of the Popes and that of the " Sawdust Cæsar " is working in full harmony in Spain, a fact to which it will be necessary to recur subsequently. Enough evidence has already accumulated to demonstrate that, just as Henry IV of France abjured his Protestant creed on the principle that " Paris was worth a Mass ", so Mussolini, in order to gain the support of the Catholic Church against the international movement of Socialism and Democracy, has abjured his atheism on similar grounds. The two heirs of that great slave-holding Empire of antiquity, the Rome of the Cæsars, unite to prevent the modern emancipation of mankind

---

[1] *Cf.* An article by Edith Moore, *The Political Face of Rome*, in the " Socialist Vanguard ", October, 1936.

[2] See Note BB, page 200.

from servitude. The lictors' rods precede the Cross, the white surplice of the priest conceals the black shirt of the Fascist, holy water mingles with castor oil to brew a new opiate for the people. Italian Fascism, the prototype of World Fascism, points the way towards an alliance on an international scale.

Note AA : *Mussolini on Religion, Then and now*

In July 1904 there appeared at Genoa a pamphlet entitled *Man and the Divinity*—" L'Homme et la Divinité "—by Benito Mussolini. Under the title *God does not exist* it was subsequently circulated by Italian anarchists in the U.S.A. The first and last paragraphs will suffice to give a resumé of its contents :

" When we claim that God does not exist we mean to deny by this declaration the personal God of theology, the God worshipped in various ways and divers modes by believers the world over, that God who from nothing created the Universe, from chaos matter, that God of absurd attributes who is an affront to human reason. With each new discovery of chemistry, physics, biology, the anthropological sciences, of the practical application of sound principles, dogma collapses. It is a part of that old edifice of religion which crumbles and falls in ruins. The continuous progress of the natural sciences now extending from city to country, disperses the darkness of the Middle Ages, and the

multitudes desert the churches where from generation to generation they betook themselves to pray
to God—that monstrous product of human ignorance. Let us examine the nature of God. We
force ourselves therefore to reason in a vacuum,
the God of religions being their own image of their
mental vacuum, the proof of the complete absence
of any activity in reasoning. . . .

" . . . If we read the history of religions, we
find that it deals with the pathology of the human
brain. If to-day the Middle Ages are retiring
into the thick shadows of convents, it is due to
triumphant scepticism, and if the epidemic disease
of religion no longer appears with the terrible
intensity of former times, it is due to the diminu-
tion of the political power of the church, which
formerly placed on the heads of people its cap of
lead.

" Religion presents itself to our eyes in another
characteristic, the atrophy of reason. The faculty
by which man is differentiated from the lower
animals is his reasoning power. But the devout
believer renounces reason, refuses to explain the
things which surround him, the innumerable natural
phenomena, because his religious faith is enough
for him. The brain loses the habit of thinking,
and this religious sottishness hurls mankind back
into animalism.

" In concluding we say that religious man is an
abnormality and that religion is the certain cause
of epidemic diseases of the mind which require
the care of alienists.

" Religion has shown itself in the open as the
institution whose aim is political power by which

to externalize the exploitation and the ignorance of the people." [1]

Such, in 1904, were the views of the present protector of the Apostles, of the " man raised up by God ". They may advantageously be compared with the present views of Mussolini on religion and Fascism outlined above. In 1932 " Fascism venerates the God of the Saints, ascetics and heroes ", but in 1904 " the history of many Saints beatified by the Church is repugnant. It shows nothing more than a profound aberration of the human spirit in search of ultra-terrestrial chimeras ; it is a delirium which can attain the state of spasms, of passion which ends in madness. Therefore, many of those who to-day hover over the altars of the Catholic church are pathological cases, hysterics and demoniacs ". It may be added that, in his official autobiography, Mussolini records that his chief pre-occupation at this stage of his career was grief at the death of his mother !

Note BB

In his Encyclical on Foreign Missions, *Maximum Illud*, of November 30, 1919—Benedict XV (1914-22) wrote :

" It is a matter of genuine sorrow that there still exist countries to which the Catholic Faith was brought centuries ago, but where, in spite of that fact, one does not find even now native priests, except possibly those occupying minor posts . . . The native priest understands better than any

[1] George Seldes, *Sawdust Caesar*, American Edition, pp. 389-390, the translation is by Mr. Seldes.

outsider how to proceed with his own people ".
The Pope then laid it down as axiomatic that
Catholicism must always aim at acclimatizing itself
among native races, and could only do this by
shedding its foreign associations. Curiously enough,
it was Pope Pius XI, later the Pope of the Lateran
Treaty and the Abyssinian War, who, after quoting
the above words of his predecessor in his own
Encyclical on Missions, *Rerum Ecclesiae*, Feb. 28,
1926, added these prophetic words :

" Moreover, the foreign missionary, because of
his imperfect knowledge of the language, often
finds himself embarrassed when he attempts to
express his thoughts, with the result that the
force and efficacy of his preaching are thereby
greatly weakened. In addition to the afore-
mentioned difficulties there are others which must
always be taken into account. Let us suppose,
for example, that either because of the fortunes
of war, or because of certain political happenings
in a mission field, the ruling government is changed
in that territory and that the new government decrees or requests that the missionaries of a certain
nationality be expelled; or let us suppose that
the inhabitants of a particular territory, having
reached a fairly high degree of civilization and at
the same time a corresponding development in
civil and social life, and desiring to become free
and independent, should drive away from their
country the governor, the soldiers, the missionaries
of the foreign nation to whose rule they are subject.
All this, of course, cannot be done without violence.
Everyone can see what great harm would accrue
to the Church in that land in the circumstances,

unless a native clergy had been spread beforehand throughout the country like a network and were, by consequence, in a position to provide adequately for the population which had been converted to Christ."

The issue of this encyclical was followed up by the ordination of six Chinese bishops, and one Japanese bishop in St Peter's, Rome, in 1929. In the light of the above principles and actions it is evident that the Papal policy of endorsing the actions of Fascist Imperialism among the coloured races is one fraught with danger to the future of Roman Catholicism as a world religion. The Pope's own words quoted above themselves rise up against him.

(b) THE PAPACY AND GERMAN FASCISM

Undoubtedly the most powerful Fascist régime in the contemporary world is that represented by Hitler and the " National Socialist " (Nazi) Party in Germany. While Hitler personally lacks the lucid and cynical intellect of Mussolini, Germany's greater military and political strength enables her to play a more decisive part in contemporary affairs, and to loom larger in the world. Whereas formerly by " Fascism " the world meant Italy, nowadays the primacy passes more and more, to German Fascism ; Hitler, not Mussolini, is now the symbol of contemporary political reaction and cultural atavism.

From the standpoint of the religious reaction and of its leader, the Papacy, Fascist Germany has a particular importance, since Germany alone of the Fascist Empires is in a position to conduct a crusade in defence of "Christian Civilization" against the great anti-Christian State, Soviet Russia, whose conversion or destruction is a *sine qua non* for the future political and spiritual domination of Europe by the Fascist-Clerical combination.

At one time, as is well known, Rome was not unfavourably disposed to the Soviets, despite their professed atheism, since the Bolshevik Revolution had broken the power of the Russian Orthodox Church, the ancient rival of Rome since the failure of the Jesuits to instal a Catholic Tsar in the days of the "False Demetrius" (1605). The Vatican originally hoped that the new Russian régime would provide an opportunity for Roman Catholicism to fill the vacant space.[1] When, however, it found that Bolshevism had come to stay and could not be converted, its destruction became necessary as an indispensable prerequisite to the spiritual enslavement of Europe. Germany, whose military strength and geographical position alone enables her to attempt this feat, is therefore of decisive importance in the Papal scheme of things.

An alliance with German Fascism is, in fact, the pivotal point of the whole scheme. None the less, certain local features peculiar to German Fascism, have hitherto obstructed this alliance, and prevented us from being able to describe it, up to the present time, as more than a tendency.

German Fascism came to power amid the throes

[1] See Note CC, p. 209.

of an anti-Bolshevik campaign in which the Catholic
Church was extremely active. Even in the days of
the Hohenzollern Empire 1871-1918—German
Catholicism, organized politically in the " Centre
Party ", worked intensively to combat the spread
of Socialist and Rationalist ideas. It is common
knowledge that, as far back as 1878, German
Catholicism waged the celebrated *Kulturkampf*
against the whole strength of the Hohenzollern
Empire, and successfully withstood the assaults of
Bismarck, then at the height of his power, eventually compelling him to " go to Canossa " (1887).
Under the Weimar Republic (1918-33) the Catholic
" Centre " several times governed Germany in
coalition with other parties. The Vatican is
accordingly no stranger to German politics, and
has for long regarded Socialism in that country
as the outstanding menace which must be defeated
at all costs.

To understand the relations that have hitherto
existed between the Catholic Church and the
Hitler State it is necessary, above all, to bear
the foregoing in mind. At all costs the menace of
Bolshevism must be defeated ; this is the cardinal
axiom of the Roman Catholic hierarchy in Germany,
near enough to Russia for its contagion to spread
West, and long familiar with Socialism in an
aggressively anti-Christian form. A Catholic prelate has described the anti-religious campaign which,
prior to Hitler's advent to power in January, 1933,
was carried on by such organizations as the German
Communist Party and its auxiliary organization,
the " Association of Proletarian Freethinkers ".
Nor should it be forgotten that the former German

Social Democratic Party, moderate as were its political opinions in most respects, was definitely anti-Christian and aggressively anti-clerical.[1]

To appraise the relations hitherto existing between Rome and German Fascism, it is above all necessary to bear the above facts in mind. *The* fundamental enemies of both Catholicism and Fascism in Germany are the same; Socialism, Bolshevism and Freethought (In German Fascist circles, cultural atavism, the struggle against modern ideas has gone much further than elsewhere). This overmastering bond of a common enemy makes it certain that, eventually, the political alliance between Catholicism and the Hitler State will be consummated and evidenced in action. In this respect, the " Crusade " at present being conducted in Spain by German troops with the blessing and active support of the Church supplies a reliable foretaste of what will presently occur elsewhere and on a larger scale.[2]

At the same time, the classic definition of the word "tendency", already cited, is exactly applicable to the past and present relations of German Fascism and Catholicism; the movement, ultimately irresistible, towards an eventual alliance has been " checked and retarded " by certain counter-tendencies, peculiar to the Nazi movement. For, while German Fascism originally arose in Catholic Germany, and its headquarters, prior to 1933, were in Munich, the capital of Germany's most Catholic State, yet Nazism inherited certain pre-Christian doctrines which for long inhibited cordial relations with Rome.

[1] *Cf.* Mgr. M. d'Herbigny, Bishop of Ilium, *Militant Atheism.*
[2] See section on Spain below, p. 212.

Apart from the irritating claims of " Totalitarianism ", which have already caused friction in Italy, German Fascism, unlike Italian, professed an intolerant cult of " Aryan " racial prejudice, which included both active anti-Semitism and a semi-official encouragement to the " German Christians "—representing a Christianity divorced from all Jewish traits, that is, from its own history— and even to the primitive neo-pagan cults of Odin, Thor, and the Solar Wheel, associated with General Ludendorff and Professor Hauer.

Such attitudes are, naturally, quite irreconcilable with Roman Catholicism, which is international beyond any possibility of compromise, and did not oppose Luther in the interests of an " Aryan " Jesus, or condemn Galileo's views on the Solar System in order to instal the worship of the Solar Wheel ! [1]

As a result of the Nazi activities there has been constant friction between the Hitler State and the German Hierarchy, and the Papal concordat with Germany has not, as yet, borne its full fruits. None the less, as the war against Socialism is a necessity to both parties, whereas neo-Paganism and the cult of the Aryan " Superman " are merely romantic sidelines from the standpoint of the Nazis themselves, it may be confidently inferred that an alliance between the most reactionary Fascist Empire and the most reactionary Christian Church will eventually be formed for the purpose, absolutely indispensable to both, of carrying on the common fight against modern civilization in its

[1] See Note DD, p. 210.

inseparable twin forms of Socialism and Scientific Rationalism.[1]

At present (early in 1937) events in Spain, by raising the " spectre of communism ", appear to be bringing that alliance appreciably nearer. As pointed out below, the political and ideological interests of Papal Rome and of Berlin coincide in Spain. Hitler assumes openly the rôle of defender of " Christian civilization " against the menace of " Asiatic " Bolshevism. To meet this " Asiatic " peril, he concludes on alliance with those " good Europeans ", the Japanese, now officially recognized as " Aryans " by the phrenologists and other " scientists " of the Third Reich. As the Papacy traditionally claims the same rôle as Hitler, the Catholic Church and the Hitler State are now the Siamese twins of the contemporary European Reaction.

Both parties now appear to recognize that this is so. At the annual Nazi Conference at Nuremberg in September, 1936, anti-Soviet pronouncements were the order of the day. They were echoed at the ensuing conference of Catholic bishops at Fulda, which declared that the national power of resistance to Bolshevism should be strengthened and settled by an early restoration of religious peace. The longer the Spanish civil war goes on, the sooner is this likely to come about. The " providential " rôle of the Führer is already recognized by the Catholic Church. In any proximate

[1] The Concordat between the Vatican and Germany was signed on July 20, 1933, by Cardinal Eugenio Pacelli, Papal Secretary of State, and Franz von Papen, Hitler's predecessor as Imperial Chancellor, and ratified on Sept. 10 of that year. Von Papen is a Catholic, as, nominally, at least, is Hitler himself.

war against "Godless" Russia or backsliding France, the Third Reich can rely on the moral and political support of the Vatican. That much is already quite certain.

Even before the outbreak of the present Spanish Civil War an editorial in the (English) *Catholic Times* put the matter concisely :

"Perhaps after all the Pope was right to be patient with the crudities of jejune Fascism, to be patient even now with the excesses of Nazism. . . . He has borne with insults in Italy, with fanaticism and persecution in Germany, and has refused to break with Italy even over the Abyssinian question, because he sees that Fascism, Nazism and Imperialism, though their excesses are evil, are in any case an incomparably smaller evil than Communism.

"Our mission of salvation to Europe is to establish a united anti-Communist Front. We must restore friendly relations with Italy and Germany, even at a great sacrifice, and then induce France, which will not be difficult, to fall into line with us, on grounds of political safety." [1]

The above quotation puts the political attitude of Catholicism with regard to contemporary Europe in a nutshell. As the anti-Socialist front desired by the Catholic Church is unthinkable without the active participation of Hitler and the Third Reich, the alliance between these arch-enemies of modern progress may be already said to be as good as in

[1] See the *Catholic Times*, June 26, 1936, cited by Edith Moore *ut supra*.

being. The Holy Alliance of contemporary re-action without either Hitler or the Pope, would be *Hamlet* without the Prince of Denmark. This funda-mental necessity ensures their mutual inclusion and active co-operation in the Crusade against modern civilization as manifested and summed up in the contemporary movement towards political, economic, cultural, and religious emancipation, that finds expression in the present phase of social evolution.

The present friction in Germany does not con-tradict the above. It only requires the Hitler State to be threatened with destruction from below for the alliance to be renewed. A " Red " Germany would be the end both of European Fascism and Catholicism.

Note CC : The Papacy and Bolshevism

In the summer of 1922 the King of Italy enter-tained the delegates to the Genoa Conference on board his yacht. At this function the Cardinal Archbishop of Genoa was sitting next to Chicherin, at that time Soviet Minister of Foreign Affairs. The Archbishop expressed the greatest interest in the Russian experiment, and was, in particular, favourably impressed by Mr Chicherin's assurances that the Bolshevik régime intended to carry the principle of the " Free Church in the Free State " to its logical conclusion of complete religious toleration, unknown in Tsarist Russia, where the Roman Catholic Church, like other dissenting bodies, felt the heavy hand of the intolerant "orthodox" Russian Church and laboured under many legal and social disabilities.[1]

Since 1922 the professed atheism of the Soviet Union and the world-wide campaign against religion carried on by it in conjunction with the Communist International has converted Rome into an implacable enemy. This campaign is analyzed in its international bearings by the Vatican "expert" on Russia, Mgr. M. d'Herbigny, Bishop of Ilium, in his book *Militant Atheism—the World-wide Propaganda of Communism*. *Cf.* The statement of Cardinal Gasparri that the Russian Revolution was a judgment on Tsarism for its treatment of Roman Catholicism. *Cf.* Colonel Repington—*The First World War*, Vol. 2, p. 440. The above statement was made to Repington himself.

Note DD : *Catholicism and Neo-Paganism*

In 1933 Cardinal Faulhaber, Archbishop of Munich, preached a series of sermons in which he denounced anti-Semitism, the "Aryan" cult, and the idealization of the "great blonde beasts", the German tribes of antiquity.[2] Internationalism is, of course, a first principle of Catholicism, which she could not possibly abandon ; she could never accept a "German Jesus".

As regards the neo-Pagan cults, these are so

[1] *Cf.* Louis Fischer, *The Soviets in World Affairs.*

[2] Cardinal von Faulhaber, *Judaism, Christianity and Germany.*

fantastic and out of touch with modern life that, unless Fascism can conduct Europe back to barbarism in a new Dark Age, it is impossible for them to have any future. Odin, Thor and the Solar Wheel belong to the nomadic social state of forest tribes such as were the ancient Germans of the Dark Ages. Their table manners unfit them for modern society! To restore these cults to effectual life to-day, it would be necessary to restore pre-industrial, pre-technical conditions of life. To see the absurdity of this, we have only to visualize the future of so militaristic a State as Nazi Germany without either machine guns or Krupp's. In that case, the triumph of the " Red Asiatics ", armed, however, with the weapons provided by Western science, would be speedy and overwhelming, as that stalwart high priest of Odin, General Ludendorff, at least, ought to know! Along with the Solar Wheel, the emblem of forest Paganism, the Neo-Pagans should advocate " back to the bow and arrow "! This, however, would not be a popular doctrine in present-day Germany, which is keenly alive to progress, at least in the sphere of military technique, and, however much it may admire those " Nordic heroes " Alaric, Genseric, Hengist and Horsa, would scarcely relish returning to their military methods even to oblige Professor Hauer and Co. One cannot consider Neo-Paganism either as a serious force in itself or as likely to prove a difficult obstacle to the Catholic-Fascist alliance of the future.

(c) THE PAPACY AND SPANISH FASCISM

1. *The Church in Spanish History*

Up to the present time by far the clearest, most open, and most striking example of the Fascist-Catholic Alliance is furnished by the events occurring at the time of writing in Spain. The Holy Alliance of the Papal Church and the Dictator State is there displayed in the most naked and aggressive form possible. In Spain, the classic land of Catholic intolerance, the native soil of those champions of the " Church militant here on earth ", St Dominic, Torquemada and St Ignatius Loyola, the war between mediævalism and modern civilization is now displaying itself clearly and unmistakably. South of the Pyrenees we can already see in a microcosm the future of the macrocosm, Western civilization, if the Clerical-Totalitarian alliance is permitted to work itself out to its logical conclusion. For this reason, it is incumbent on the student of the Holy Alliance of the twentieth century to devote special attention to this phenomenon of contemporary history. We begin, accordingly, by tracing the roots of the Catholic domination in Spanish history.

The connexion between Catholicism and Spain dates from Roman times. It was the bigoted Spanish soldier, Theodosius—by courtesy of ecclesiastical historians " the Great "—who, rather than the latitudinarian Constantine, was really responsible for the triumph of Catholic Christianity in the Roman Empire; it was above all Theodosius who introduced Europe to the twelve centuries of ferocious persecution which marked the long ascendancy of the Catholic Church (379-95).

With the conversion of the Gothic kings to Catholicism after the fall of the Roman Empire (589) the Church became the greatest landowner in Spain, and at the time of the Arab-Moorish invasion owned, it is computed, not far short of half of the land in the country. Its intolerance, an endemic characteristic of Spanish Catholicism, was manifested by ferocious persecutions of the Jews. As early as the end of the seventh century, St Julian, Archbishop of Toledo, set forth the ideal of an all-Catholic Spain and strove to extirpate Judaism altogether.

It is now known that the Arab conquest (711-12) could hardly have taken place without this intolerance. The Mohammedan invaders originally came to Spain as mercenaries in a Spanish Civil War, a familiar rôle to-day. It was the degeneracy of the country and the active assistance given to them by the Jews, who opened the cities to them, that enabled the Arabs to conquer it with a minimum effort. Thanks to this assistance, while they came as mercenaries, they remained as conquerors. Under Mohammedan rule, as Mr McCabe has convincingly shown, Spain enjoyed several centuries of civilization, economic prosperity and religious tolerance, a unique interlude in her gloomy history throughout both ancient and modern times.[1]

In 1492, after a prolonged struggle which ex-

[1] Joseph McCabe, *The Splendour of Moorish Spain*.

tended over several centuries, the " Moors " were finally defeated, and their last stronghold, the Alhambra of Granada, survived into an alien age to testify to the superiority of the vanished civilization over the fanatical clerical Imperialism which succeeded it. For the victorious Spaniards lost no time in abandoning alike the humanistic culture which formed the basis for the fine Arab civilization of the Middle Ages, at the same time as they neglected the admirable system of irrigation which formed the indispensable foundation of the economic well-being that Spain had enjoyed under the Mohammedan régime.

The land of Spain eventually went to rack and ruin along with the brain of the Spanish nation. Since the end of the sixteenth century Spain had been increasingly a physical and mental desert. The modern history of the Spanish nation from that date to the most recent times was described by Karl Marx with penetrating insight, when he spoke of " the inglorious and slow decay " which had slowly strangled Spain in the past three centuries, and had converted the natural El Dorado of Roman and Arab days into the huge rural slum that is Modern Spain.

The Decline and Fall of the Spanish Empire —1492-1898—parallels in its long-drawn-out agony and its mournful and gloomy story of squalid yet tragic splendour the classical drama etched in masterly outline by Gibbon, of the Decline and Fall of the Roman Empire, to which majestic ruin the Spanish débacle of modern times furnishes the nearest historic counterpart.

Expressed in its essentials, the story of that

imposing ruin, modern Spain, can be traced back
to two fatal gifts placed by its evil fairy in the
cradle of the newly-liberated Spanish people as
they emerged from African domination, gifts which
have crushed Spain, both physically and mentally,
from that day to this. That evil Fairy is the Church
of Rome, which, at the close of the fifteenth century,
presented her with an Empire which she could
not govern and an Inquisition which she could
not shake off. In 1478 the Dominican, Torquemada,
erected the Spanish Inquisition on models supplied
by Rome, and the reigning Pope, Alexander VI
—a Spaniard of Moorish descent, Rodrigo Borgia—
bestowed on Spain the New World Empire just
discovered by Columbus. (1493)

Spain consumed her external energies throughout
the sixteenth century both in conquering the Empire
which the Papacy had so kindly " given " her,
and in repaying the debt by a century-long war
for the reconquest of Protestant Europe in the
interests of Rome, in which the Spanish army
worked hand in hand with the Jesuits. Meanwhile, the internal energies of Spain were consumed by the ruthless strangulation of the intellectual life of the Spanish nation, by the Inquisition,
which drove out both Moors and Jews, exterminated the Protestant Reformers, eradicated any
liberal tendencies in the Spanish Church (the
philosophy of Descartes and Bacon was interdicted
in the Spanish Universities down to the end of
the eighteenth century), and, in addition, assisted
the kings to crush out of existence the original
parliamentary institutions of Spain in favour of a
stifling and artificially centralized royal despotism.

Spain collapsed under this double strain, and is only now beginning to recover from the consequent decay that set in on the morrow of her titanic efforts in the sixteenth century.[1]

In his monumental *History of Civilization* T. H. Buckle thus characterizes the decay :

" The victory gained by the Church increased her power and influence. During the rest of the seventeenth century, not only were the interests of the clergy deemed superior to the interests of laymen, but the interests of the layman were scarcely thought of. . . .

" No one enquired, no one doubted, no one presumed to ask if all this was right. The minds of men succumbed and were prostrate. While every other country was advancing, Spain alone was receding. Every other country was making some addition to knowledge, creating some art, or enlarging some science. Spain, numbed into a deathlike torpor, spell-bound and entranced by the accursed superstition which preyed on her strength, presented to Europe a solitary instance of constant decay. For her no hope remained ; and before the close of the seventeenth century the only question was by whose hands the blow should be struck which would dismember that once mighty Empire, whose shadow had covered the world, and whose vast remains were imposing even in their ruin."

Buckle goes on to give some astounding figures to illustrate the decay. Between 1600 and 1700

[1]See Note EE, p. 233.

the population of Madrid fell from 400,000 to 200,000; during the same period the looms of Seville fell from 16,000 to 300, while the population dropped by 75 per cent. The woollen manufactories of Toledo fell from 50 to 13; Burgos, during the same period, became so depopulated that a contemporary declared it had lost everything except its name. In 1656 there were not enough sailors to man the fishing fleets. Even the Spanish army, in the sixteenth century the finest in Europe, was finally dragged down by the all-pervading economic decay. After its defeat by the French General Condé at Rocroy in 1643, the Spanish infantry, the former terror of Europe, sank into insignificance. Her navy, which had once enjoyed such supremacy as for long to give its name to the Atlantic " the Spanish Main ", and which added to the English language the word " Armada ", had become completely impotent to protect her American Empire, which remained only nominally Spanish throughout the eighteenth century, on account of her virtual subordination to France, to whom her Bourbon kings reduced her to political vassalage by the " Family Compact " which followed upon the " War of the Spanish Succession " (1701-13), fought to decide whether Spain was to move into the political orbit of England or of France.

Meanwhile, however, the Church retained and accentuated her stranglehold on Spain. In 1608 even the subservient Spanish Cortes (Parliament) complained that not a day passed without a layman being deprived of his property in favour of the Church. Priests and beggars, in fact, multiplied together into their subsequent rôle of twin landmarks of normal Spanish society. Concurrently, the fires of the Inquisition burned with a regularity which no perpetual flame tended by a Vestal Virgin could ever have surpassed. How many victims perished no one knows, but a four-figure total for a single year was not unheard-of, or even, it seems, uncommon. Still more serious was the loss in quality. From 1500 to 1800 originality in Spain was regarded as a fit subject for arson. It had an incendiary quality ! [1]

" The king, master of all lives and property, was only the servant of bishops, friars and familiars. The kings of Spain, except the first Bourbons, were nothing but servants of the Church. In no country has been seen so palpably as this one the solidarity between Church and State. Religion succeeded in living without the kings, but the kings could not exist without religion."

The first shock to this blind-alley civilization of clerical stagnation was given by the French invasion and occupation of Spain in 1808-13. While the French deprived the Spaniards of their kings and their art galleries, they also abolished the Inquisition and the *auto da fè*. Even after the downfall of Napoleon it proved impossible for the effete Bourbon dynasty, restored by English bayonets, to renew these mediæval relics. It proved equally impossible for the restored Spanish monarchy to recover its American colonies.

From 1814 to 1931, the Spanish Empire, a centre without a periphery, has rotted in a stagnant pool of political, economic and cultural atavism. The

---

[1] *Cf.* Blasco Ibanez, *In the Shadow of the Cathedral*, p. 215.

weak liberal movement has merely added insult
to injury by exposing the evils of an absolute and
anachronistic régime which it was not strong
enough to overthrow, or even challenge to any
serious extent, though the fact that both parliamentary institutions and the very word " liberal "
came originally from Spain would seem to demonstrate that the Spaniard is not such a " natural "
reactionary as is sometimes supposed.

The " left " forces had one brief interlude of
power in 1868-1874, when Spain experimented
first with a constitutional monarchy, and then with
a republic. The first Spanish Republic collapsed
under the internal strain of its own centrifugal
forces, and the clerical monarchy, bolstered up
by bayonets, brutality, and economic and cultural
backwardness, continued its inglorious career down
to 1931, losing, *en route*, its last remnants of Empire,
the Philippine Islands and Cuba, in that ignominious
fiasco of 1898 dignified by the name of the Spanish-
American " War ". The Monarchy, however,
managed to totter on for another generation before
throne and altar were at last confronted by the
ubiquitous crisis of the twentieth century.

(2) *The Republic and the Church*

The downfall of the Bourbon monarchy in Spain
was ultimately due to its own rottenness rather than
to the strength of opposition to the Crown. The
disastrous war against Abd-El-Krim in Morocco
and the military dictatorship of General Primo
de Rivera (1923-30) were symptoms rather than

causes of the final collapse. No revolution proved necessary to get rid of Alfonso XIII ; an adverse municipal vote proved sufficient to overthrow the last autocratic king in Europe, only a few years after the novelist Blasco Ibanez, in his *Alfonso XIII Unmasked*, had drawn a terrible picture of a political régime which had long been a grotesque anomaly in the twentieth century. The second Spanish Republic, with a moderately " left " political outlook, succeeded to power.

The kings of Spain had always ruled as the nominees of the Catholic Church. Now the king had gone, but the Church remained. Prior to the present Civil War, the problem of Church versus State was the central one for the Republic. For, south of the Pyrenees, the Catholic Church retained many of the political, economic, and cultural rights which it had enjoyed universally throughout its heyday in the Middle Ages. Nothing is further from the philosophy of the Spanish Church than the modern conception of religion as a private matter, the " free Church in the Free State ", a conception forced even on the Roman Catholic Church by world conditions in countries more politically developed and technically advanced.

Far from endorsing such an outlook, the Spanish Church held vast property, was still powerful in cultural and educational matters, and worked actively in the political arena to safeguard its all-pervading influence. In 1931 the Spanish property of the Jesuit Order had a value of six thousand million pesetas (£150,000,000). As late as 1909 it had been strong enough to secure the judicial murder of the anarchist and pioneer of secular education, Francisco Ferrer; and when, a few years later, a Spanish prelate congratulated the Protestant king of Sweden on the toleration accorded to Catholics in that country, the King replied, truthfully enough, that he wished he could say the same about the treatment accorded to Protestants in Spain, where their public worship was barely legal. Down to 1868 the Roman Catholic Church was the only legally recognized religious cult in Spain, and when toleration came it was always grudging and partial.

In fact, the economic and cultural backwardness of Spain, where industry was undeveloped and illiteracy embraced nearly half the population, permitted the retention of mediæval conditions, and down to 1931 imposed on the slow growth of a backward country the crushing burden of the " dead hand " of a semi-mediæval church.[1]

The Republic at first set to work with considerable energy to tackle this problem, whose solution was, ultimately, a question of its own self-preservation. In the first, radical, phase of the republic, Church and State were officially separated, the Jesuit Order, always powerful and active in the land of its birth, was dissolved, and not only did the Church lose its State subsidy, but its property rights were severely curtailed, both by legislation directed against clerical participation in industry, and by the agrarian reforms projected by the first Azana government. These measures led

---

[1] As late as 1851 the concordat with Rome laid it down : " The Catholic Apostolic Roman religion, to the exclusion of every other cult, continues to be the sole religion of the Spanish nation."

the Vatican to take strong action. In June 1933 Pope Pius XI issued an encyclical condemning the separation of Church and State, and excommunicating the members of the government in quite mediæval fashion. While it is customary nowadays to compare every revolution to the Russian revolution of 1917, the first phase of the Spanish Revolution actually bore a far closer resemblance to the Mexican Revolution, which similarly drew down upon it a wrathful encyclical from Pius XI. In Mexico the revolution was likewise a movement of the modern spirit and the anti-clerical political Left. As in Spain, its fight was waged against a political Church, an oligarchy of big landowners closely allied with the Church, and generally against mediæval conditions of life. The Mexican agrarian, anti-clerical, revolution was undoubtedly the immediate prototype and model of the second Spanish Republic, offspring of a similar culture and of similar social, economic, and religious conditions.[1]

In questions of politics the Roman Church has always been a very adaptable institution, and the threat to its long-established monopoly induced even the mediævalist Spanish Church to bring its political technique at least up to date. As Spain was, at long last, moving towards the conditions of the modern world, even the Church had to adapt itself to modern political conditions in the world of the twentieth century, and to find a broader basis for its rule than its traditional alliance with parasitic grandees and reactionary generals. Consequently the Church, and, particularly the Jesuits,

[1] See E. J. Dillon, *President Obregon—A World Reformer.*

identified themselves with the " Catholic Action " Party, led by Gil Robles, a clever demagogue, who had studied the propaganda technique of Hitler and Mussolini.

Robles soon became a powerful force in Spanish politics, and was mainly responsible for the series of Right-Wing governments which, between June, 1933 and the victory of the Popular Front in February 1936, slowed down the forward movement of the Spanish Republic, and in particular reduced the anti-clerical legislation of early republican days to a legal farce. Robles, liberally supplied with clerical funds, organized the first mass party which the Spanish reaction had ever found it necessary to use. He worked openly for the union of the Right-Wing parties, and his own programme, very similar to that of Dollfüss in Austria, represented a combination of Fascist demagogy, clerical traditionalism, and generally an ultra-Right programme disguised under the Left phrases which modern conditions render necessary.

After the suppression of the rising of the Asturias miners in October, 1934, Gil Robles became the most powerful man in Spain. As Minister of War (May-December 1935) he brought into the General Staff crypto-Fascists like General Franco, and drew closer the alliance between Fascism, the Army, the Catholic Church, and the reactionary classes in Spanish society. For a moment it looked as if the Church had gained its ends by purely political action, and that it would remain the real power behind the scenes under a conservative republic, as formerly under the monarchy, and without recourse to civil war.

The victory of the " Popular Front " in the elections of February, 1936 upset these bright prospects of peaceful penetration. The return of a " Left " government to power under the anticlerical radical Azana foreshadowed both the enforcement of the existing laws against the Church, so far inoperative, and a resolute policy of agrarian reform so as to make an end, in Spain as in Mexico, of the great estates (*Haciendas*) and of their proclerical owners, the Spanish grandees. Besides, who knew where the Left would stop, particularly since it is proverbial that " appetite comes with eating " ? For the Church to rule Spain, her traditional society must be retained. As political action had failed, nothing was left but civil war. The time had come for the Catholic-Fascist alliance to come out into the open and to display itself in its true colours for all the world to see.

(3) *The Catholic Church and the Civil War*

The present Spanish Civil War was started on July 18, 1936 by the rising of the army in Africa under the command of General Francisco Franco, former Chief of Staff to Gil Robles. At the time of writing it is still raging without fortune having thus far inclined to either side.

Civil War in Spain is no new thing ; Madrid was also beleaguered a century ago. What, however, distinguishes the present Civil War in Spain from all the preceding civil wars in Spanish history, indeed from all European wars since the epoch of the French Revolution, is that it is not only a war of interests, but also of ideologies: it is a "religious" war in the sense that it marks the opening of an era of wars in which the combatants are divided not only, nor even chiefly, by bonds of interest or race, but by ties of opinion and sentiment; it represents the clash of two rival and irreconcilable world-philosophies.

In this sense the Civil War now raging in Spain may possess an epochal character as the precursor and prototype of a whole era of wars of ideology, or, using the word in a rather loose sense, of an epoch of religious wars; that is, of wars fought, largely at least, for altruistic ends that transcend the purely material factors involved. It is quite possible that the present Spanish war marks a transition from the purely materialistic and sordid wars of the Imperialist epoch to wars of a different time, and type, wars into which ideas enter, no less than interests, and in which they transcend the material boundaries of nations. Certainly, the present Spanish War displays all the altruism, the fanaticism, and equally the ferocious cruelty which wars of such a type always engender.

In Spain, at least, the rival protagonists are clearly marked. On the one side is the "Popular Front", a somewhat heterogeneous combination of all the forces which, in one way or another, stand for social evolution and the breaking of mediæval fetters. These range from the Liberals on the right to the Anarchists—a political species elsewhere extinct—on the extreme Left. On the other side are ranged the whole force both of the Spanish reaction itself and of the reactionary Clerical-Fascist *bloc* in contemporary Europe. Moreover, volunteers from all over Europe have flocked to the banners of their respective creeds. We should need to go back to the " Thirty Years' War ", the last of the great religious wars of Europe (1618-48), to find the parallel of the polyglot armies now assembled on the Spanish front. What Europe looks like becoming to-morrow, that is Spain to-day !

If the army of the " People's Front " is the first army assembled by the forces of social evolution in the twentieth century, in fact, *the first army of the Twentieth Century* (*i.e.*, the first which reflects its spirit in action), the army of the rebel generals represents no less clearly the forces of the contemporary reaction. A glance at its constituent elements suffices to make this plain.

The army of General Franco, the army of mediævalism in Church and State, consists of the following elements :

(1) Foreign mercenaries, chiefly Moors. The only creed that these would seem to possess is that of all mercenaries at all times ; the creed brilliantly summarized by the sixteenth century Swiss in the formula : " No money, no Swiss." It may be pointed out, however, that the essentially artificial character of the Spanish reaction is demonstrated by the use of Mohammedan barbarians to defend " Christian civilization ", and of the traditional enemies of Spain to defend " integral nationalism ".

(2) Royalists, who want the return of " the most Catholic King ", and of the Church which always pulled the wires behind its royal puppets.

(3) The Carlists—Traditionalists—for whom even the régime of Alfonso XIII was too modern, and

who preferred a " legitimist " monarchy, one even more reactionary and subservient to the Church.[1]

(4) The Fascist-Clerical followers of Gil Robles, whose aim is a " Christian State "—*i.e.* a " corporate " State, run on Fascist lines, but subservient to the Church. Robles would probably prefer to keep the form of a Republic, as this is better adapted to demagogic purposes than is an openly reactionary monarchy.

(5) German and Italian troops sent by Hitler and Mussolini with the dual object of checking the spread of socialism and democracy in Southern Europe, and of securing a military and economic vassal who can be relied on to support the Fascist Powers in the event of a European War.

(6) Volunteers from nations such as Ireland and Portugal, actuated partly by hatred of " Communism ", or in reality of the modern spirit, and partly by fanatical devotion to the Roman Catholic Church.

Such are the constituent elements in the " United Front " behind Franco. His backers embody his programme.

When we turn to the rebel leader for an explicit pronouncement of his political and cultural aims, we find nothing but promises, certainly quite definite, of the extermination of all the forces opposed to him, and vague denunciations of " class war ", etc., such as form the stock in trade of Fascist demagogues ; but on one inspired occasion General Franco indiscreetly let the cat out of the bag, and disclosed his real aims. His programme, he declared, was " the restoration of the Spain of

[1] See Note FF, p. 233.

Columbus ". (This presumably does not include the reconquest of the Spanish Empire in both hemispheres ; this would be an even more difficult enterprise than the capture of Madrid, an enterprise which is taxing the resources of the Fascists to the full!)

Considered as a social programme, this statement is an index of the Spain which would arise on the morrow of a Fascist victory. For " the Spain of Columbus " was the Spain of the " most Catholic Kings ", of Isabella " the Catholic ", who boasted that she had depopulated whole districts " for the sake of Christ and his Virgin Mother " ; the Spain that committed to " the flames which avenged the honour of God " both the writing of the Arab scientists and, when it could catch them, the scientists themselves ; the Spain in which the Grand Inquisitor, the most powerful man was that apostle of enlightment, Torquemada ; the Spain which had to be bribed by the gold of the Indies to admit that the world was round, and, to obtain that gold, exterminated the aborigines of the West Indies within a single generation, baptizing the " heathen " infants first, and then dashing out their brains. Such is the real historic Spain which the present Spanish reaction would restore, if it could exterminate the upholders of the modern spirit with the aid of its foreign allies and its barbaric mercenaries.[1]

In Spain, indeed, we have the classic example which history has so far afforded of the new Holy Alliance in operation, of Fascism and militarism working openly hand in glove with Roman

[1] See *The Truth About Columbus,* by Charles Duff.

Catholicism and mediævalism. It is common knowledge that without the support of the Fascist powers
the rebellion of Franco would have been crushed
at the outset; in such an event it would probably
not have lasted longer than the abortive pro-
nunciamento of General Sanjurjo in Seville in 1932.
If Franco wins, he will become a German and
Italian puppet, propped up by foreign bayonets.
Dependent on the support of a foreign prætorian
guard, he may learn the truth of the historic adage
of Count Cavour that "one can do anything with
bayonets except sit on them".

It is agreed by all observers that the only in-
digenous support the militarist Junta can rely on
in Spain, and among the Spanish people, comes
from the Church and the districts where it is still
supreme. The only parts of Spain where there
is any enthusiasm for "the Spain of Columbus"
are those which are still culturally and spiritually
in the era of Columbus, and where, accordingly,
devotion to the "national" cause is devotion to
the Middle Ages and to the Church of the Middle
Ages. Elsewhere, "the Spain of Columbus"
depends for its restoration on the return to Spain
of those same Moors whose preliminary expulsion
from Spain in the very year—1492—in which
Columbus discovered America, was the essential
preliminary to the sombre and short-lived glories
of the Spanish Empire.

The "Spain" of General Franco and his Junta
of reactionaries is, in fact, Catholic Spain, the
Spain of the Church, a Spain which could never
survive the abrupt "leap across the centuries"
which the advent to that country of any really

modern régime, which took its task seriously and
set to work in earnest to conduct it from the
seventeenth century, where it stopped dead, to
the twentieth, would involve. The effects of a
simultaneous reformation, renaissance, and revolution upon backward and priest-ridden Russia
were not happy, at least from the point of view of
the priests and the " faithful ", whose " faith "
was demolished by the advent of knowledge and
who abandoned with equal rapidity the faith, the
dirt, and the agricultural implements, which their
fathers had enjoyed from time immemorial.

A similar transformation south of the Pyrenees
explains why the Catholic Church in Spain is now
fighting for its life. It has not forgotten what
happened in Russia and in Mexico. It is after all,
no accident that the English novelist who first
predicted the Russian Revolution also predicted the
Spanish one, or that the man who actually led
the Russian Revolution had already made the
historic prophecy that " Europe would go Red
at both ends ", *i.e.* east of the Vistula and south
of the Pyrenees.[1]

So far as Spain is concerned, the civil war is a
conflict of " Rome versus Reason ". The only
hold Franco has on Spain is through the Church;
that he has to depend so largely on foreign mercenaries affords plain proof of the weakness of the
church even in its traditional citadel. In the election
which led to the Popular Front government, voters
were warned by the priests that it was a " mortal
sin " to vote even Liberal. It is said that Spanish

---

[1] *Cf.* H. Seton Merriman, *The Sowers* and *In Kedar's Tents*; L.
D. Trotsky, *Autobiography.*

Protestants have been murdered by the reactionaries, no doubt at clerical instigation, since it cannot be supposed that the Moors know enough about theology to signal them out for destruction. Spain and the Spanish intellect are on the march. Nevertheless all that Catholicism, both Spanish and foreign, can do is being done. The Pope blesses the fugitive Spanish rebels in a dissertation on the Spanish " Terror ", the Spanish hierarchy forms part of the rebel's military machine, the churches are converted into Fascist arsenals, even the Mohammedan Moors are promised entrance into the Christian paradise if they kill enough baptized Spaniards with rifles, ornamented with the insignia of the Sacred Heart of Jesus ! [1]

Nor are such efforts confined to Spanish Catholicism. The Catholic Press throughout the world is pro-Franco and pro-Fascist. After all, it could hardly give the lie direct to the infallible Pope ! The Portuguese dictatorship, kept in power by the Church, turns Portugal into a Fascist arsenal ; the Irish " Christian Front " sends an Irish brigade to Spain to join the rebels. A widely-circulated Irish pamphlet bears the expressive title *For God and Spain*. Its writer declares *inter alia* : " Were we to stand neutral or indifferent, when this last Crusade is being fought, we would deserve to go down to history as a shameless generation, helping by our silence and consent the new Crucifixion." The solidarity of international Catholicism here finds lucid expression. At the International

[1] See J. McGovern, M.P., *Why Bishops back Franco*, which reproduces a photograph of such a " holy " gun. Mr. McGovern is himself a Catholic. *Cf.* Notes EE and GG. pp. 233-5.

Eucharistic Congress at Manilla (Philippines) held in February 1937, public prayers were said for the victory of Franco. The Congress was presided over by a Cardinal Legate and was addressed by the Pope on the radio. The English Catholic hierarchy sponsors a " Catholic Times Refugee Fund " in order " to wipe out the shame of English money being given to the Reds " ; the English Catholic Press transforms itself into an arsenal of propaganda of the " corpse factory " type painfully familiar during the World War. The desperate struggle of a stunted, oppressed and thwarted people for a régime founded on reason, modern knowledge, and social justice, becomes simply an inexplicable outbreak of " Red Terror " in the jaundiced eyes of the Catholic Church.

All this is, of course, no accident. Whatever superficial non-Catholic or ill-instructed Catholic observers may think, there is nothing at all fortuitous or personal in any of these actions or the countless others that might be enumerated. Rome does not indulge in Crusades on behalf of the romantic attachments of bygone days. She is no Don Quixote—not even in Spain ! She does to-day what she must do in self-preservation. Her very existence is at stake. She cannot survive the advance of modern civilization much further. She acts in Spain to-day as she will act elsewhere to-morrow.

In Spain, in fact, we see the new Holy Alliance in the clearest light thus far available. Unless that alliance is checked, where Spain is to-day, the Western world will be to-morrow. To such a result point the indications offered by the Fascist-

Clerical Alliance in contemporary Spain. The forces of World Fascism and World Catholicism are simultaneously set in motion towards their common end, the irrevocable destruction of modern civilization in its entirety.

Note EE : The Pope and the Spanish Civil War

On Monday, September 14, 1936, Pope Pius XI received a number of refugee Spanish bishops, priests, nuns and laity, and delivered an address, subsequently published as a pamphlet by the Catholic Truth Society, the propaganda organization of English Catholicism. The ensuing verbatim extracts from the Pope's speech are sufficient to indicate his attitude, and that of the Church of which he is the head, to the events now taking place in Spain.

" All that is most fundamentally human, all that is most profoundly Divine, consecrated persons and sacred things and holy institutions, inestimable and irreplaceable treasures of faith and Christian piety as well as of culture and art, the most precious of antiquities, the holiest of relics, dignity, sanctity, the fruitful activity of lives wholly dedicated to religion, to science and to charity, the highest members of the sacred hierarchy, bishops and priests, consecrated virgins, the laity of every class and condition, venerable grey hairs and the first flower of youth, the sacred and solemn silence of the tomb itself, all has been assaulted, violated, destroyed, and in the most ruthless and barbarous ways, in an unbridled and unparalleled confusion of forces so savage and so cruel as to have been thought utterly incompatible. I do not say with human dignity, but with human nature itself, even the most miserable and debased. . . .

" One would say that a satanic preparation has rekindled, and that in our neighbour Spain, that flame of hatred and savage persecution which has been professedly reserved for the Catholic Church and the Catholic religion, as for the one real obstacle in the way of those forces which have already given proof and estimate of their quality in the attempt to subvert established order of every kind from Russia to China, from Mexico to South America.

" These attempts and preparations have been preceded and unfailingly accompanied by a universal, persistent and most astute propaganda, intent on subjecting the whole world to those absurd and disastrous ideologies which, once they have seduced and stirred up the masses, aim at nothing less than arming them, and throwing them madly against every institution human and divine."

Such are the views of the Infallible Pope on " that wicked animal which defends itself ", the legitimate and popularly elected government of Spain, when faced by an unscrupulous military rising, implemented by barbaric and pagan mercenaries.[1]

Note FF : The Carlists

When the Bourbon dynasty ascended the throne of Spain at the time of the war of the Spanish

---

[1] See " The Spanish Terror ", speech of H.H. Pope Pius XI.

Succession (1701-13) the Salic Law was introduced into Spain. Consequently no woman could
succeed to the Throne. Ferdinand VII however,
set this law aside, and left his throne by will to
his daughter Isabella (1832). The king's brother,
Don Carlos, held that his exclusion was illegal,
and a desultory civil war followed. The Carlists
or "Traditionalists" still remain in Spain, and
stand for reaction and clericalism in its extreme
form. They opposed even the limited concessions
made by the later Bourbons—under pressure—
to the modern spirit. At present, what is left of
the Carlist movement is solidly behind General
Franco.

Note GG : The Catholic Church and " Political Catholicism "

At present, an attempt is being made in English
radical circles to differentiate between the Catholic
Church as a religious institution and what is called
the "Political Catholicism" of the reactionary
Spanish clergy. It is only in a country unfamiliar
with the Church that such a mistaken conception
could arise. Thus Mr McGovern, himself a
Catholic, observes : "All my life I have opposed
the intrusion of the clergy into politics." Mr
McGovern cites similar expressions of opinion
from Spanish Catholic critics of a "political"
Church. In Spain, at least, they should know
better ; to observe the real nature of Catholicism
they have only to study the history of their own
country. Mr H. N. Brailsford, a non-Catholic,

remarks : " Catholic readers must pardon such plain speaking about this Church ; it is unique in Europe." The *Daily Herald*, official organ of the British Labour Party, remarked in an editorial, after admitting that in Spain a large part of the Hierarchy have joined the rebels :

> " they are doing so not in their capacity as Catholics, but in their capacity as anti-demon-crats, not as men of religion, but as men of politics. Surely Catholicism as a *living religious faith* (*italics in original*) has nothing to share with the men who decided to launch a disloyal and murderous attack on the people of Spain."[1]

It is obvious that all this is quite wrong and muddle-headed. There is nothing accidental about the clerical-Fascist Alliance, either in Spain or elsewhere. Those who make an illusory distinction between religious and political Catholicism have never thought the matter out nor adequately con-sidered the history and contemporary world-rôle and philosophy of the Roman Church. The Pope, at least, has no illusions, as the following passage from *The Spanish Terror* convincingly demon-strates :

> " This is to say, that where, by ways of violence or treachery according to the circumstances, by dishonesty and falsely distinguishing between the Catholic faith and political Catholicism, difficulties, obstacles, and barriers are placed in the way of full development of the action and influence of the Catholic Religion and the

[1] J. McGovern, M.P., *Why Bishops Back Franco* ; *Spain's Challenge to Labour*, H. N. Brailsford ; *Daily Herald*, August 22, 1936.

Catholic Church, in accordance with the Divine Mandate which it carries as its warrant, precisely to that extent there is aided and abetted the influence and the pernicious action of the forces of subversion." [1]

In view of the above, it is clear that Catholics who support the government, e.g. The Basques—are nationalists first and Catholics a bad second, i.e. good Nationalists but bad Catholics. Such constitute a proof of the secularization of Spanish politics.

It would be difficult to express more clearly than do these words the real " totalitarian " rôle of the Papacy as a bulwark of reaction in every sphere of contemporary life. The critics of " political " Catholicism have their answer, and from the highest authority. There is no such thing as " political " Catholicism, there never has been nor ever will be. There is only Catholicism—one and indivisible—whose action springs logically and necessarily from its theory. Whether " infallible " or not, Pope Pius XI evidently understands the real nature of Catholicism much better than do some of his British critics.

(d) *THE PAPACY AND FASCISM IN OTHER COUNTRIES*

The workings of the new Holy Alliance in the smaller countries where it operates, lack the world importance of the foregoing sections, and, generally

[1] See *The Spanish Terror*, p. 6.

speaking, repeat their outlines. It is not, accordingly, necessary to multiply superfluous detail, and the main features alone will be referred to in the following notes. The countries touched upon are, Austria, Portugal, Ireland, France and Belgium. This list is not exhaustive, and could, no doubt, be multiplied by examples from such countries as Poland, Hungary, Paraguay, etc., where clerical influence is strong and Fascist tendencies are not unknown.

1. *Austria.*

Since the Vienna massacre of Feb. 12-14, 1934, the " St Bartholomew's Eve " of modern times, a Clerical-Fascist coalition has ruled Austria, first under Dollfüss, and since his assassination by the Austrian Nazis, by Schuschnigg. Under this régime Austria has evolved a kind of Christian Fascism. Trade Unionism and party politics are alike forbidden, a corporate State is in being, public opinion is muzzled, and the only legal party is the Fascist-Catholic " Fatherland Front ". Both Dollfüss and his successor remained on the most cordial terms with the Vatican, and were themselves pious Catholics. The official title of the Republic indicates its nature : " In the name of God the Almighty from whom all right proceeds, the Austrian people receives this constitution for its Christian, German, Federal State on a corporative foundation " (Constitution of May 1, 1934). Following upon the destruction of the Socialist municipality of Vienna in February, 1934, every form, not merely of " Marxism ", but of socialist, liberal, democratic, and anti-Catholic activity is rigorously interdicted. Present-day Austria may be described succinctly as a microscopic edition of what a Fascist-Catholic Europe would be.

2. *Portugal.*

Since 1926 Portugal has lived under a Fascist-Clerical dictatorship very similar in social content to that of Austria, with a dual dictatorship of General Carmona and Professor Salazar, as President and Prime Minister respectively. A very well-informed writer has thus characterized this régime :

" Under the dictatorship, Portugal has suffered misery. Living went up by forty per cent., education was neglected, and social services were negligible. The Jesuits who had been banished from the Republic on its creation in 1910, were able to come back and comfortably reassert their old influence. The priestly class everywhere was re-established. The aspect of the Fascist régime in Portugal, about which least is known abroad, is the establishment of a political Inquisition, which works, *sub rosa*, in penal establishments. Here political prisoners are tortured in a manner which, in some respects, is more abominable than that which prevailed during the Inquisition of the Holy Catholic Church. . . . The internal espionage system of this little country costs one million pounds per annum compared with the annual £250,000 or so deemed necessary for the whole Secret Service of the British Empire.

"When a prisoner dies, he is reported to have ' committed suicide ', and the number of prison 'suicides' in contemporary Portugal is in itself enough to shake anybody's confidence in the régime that is responsible for them. Thousands of Portuguese who have shown their disapproval of this dictatorship have been sent to unsavoury parts of the tropics and placed under the charge of black troops."

Mr Prieto goes on to point out that Portugal has all along during the "non-intervention" period rendered the most active assistance possible to the Spanish rebels; a radical régime in Spain would, in point of fact, probably mean the end of this reactionary dictatorship. Hence

"Franco's revolt almost became Salazar's war. Foreign newspaper correspondents, although perfectly aware of the huddle of leaders of the Spanish revolt in the Hotel Aviz at Lisbon, scarcely troubled to keep a sharp eye on the border that touches Spain. Here the byroads of Portugal were often blocked with caravans of arms and ammunition destined for the rebels."[1]

It may be added that the political paradise described above is, far more than Germany or Italy, the direct prototype of the Burgos Junta of rebels. Both the Spanish "Left" and "Right" model themselves on Iberian examples, the Left, as indicated above, on Mexico rather than on Russia; the Right on Portugal rather than on the bigger Fascist States. The fate of the Portuguese reaction will, no doubt, depend on the ultimate issue of the civil war now raging in Spain.

[1] Carlos Prieto, *Spanish Front*, pp. 82-3.

3. *Ireland.*

Since the creation of the Irish Free State, the Catholic Church has enjoyed enormous power. In 1932 the Papal Legate at the Dublin Eucharistic Congress received a mediæval welcome. A little later the anti-religious propaganda of the Irish Communist Party was forcibly suppressed, and its offices were wrecked by the young men's league organized by " Catholic Action ". The Irish bishops control the censorship of books, and such anti-Christian works as the famous book on Christian origins by Dr Robert Eisler—*The Messiah Jesus and John the Baptist*—have been absolutely banned in Ireland. Recently the Church has actively supported and helped to organize the " Christian Front ", a body with pronounced Fascist tendencies, under General O'Duffy, who has recently led an Irish brigade to the support of General Franco. The pamphlet cited above, entitled *For God and Spain* by Aodh de Blácam, sold thirty-five thousand copies in a few weeks. As the conflict of modern civilization with mediæval-ism develops, Ireland can be relied on by the Church as an ardent member of the Holy Alliance, and any Fascist movement that grows up there must assume an aggressively Catholic tone. " The Isle of the Saints " could become a Fascist island overnight.

4. *Belgium.*

The Belgian Fascist party takes its official name —" Rexist "—from the Catholic feast of " Christ the King " (" Christus Rex "), inaugurated by

Pius XI. The "leader", Léon Degrelle, "the Belgian Hitler", is a Catholic and an ex-student at the Catholic university of Louvain. The chief strength of the Rexists is among the Flemings, the most Catholic section of the Belgian population, and Catholic influences are strong in the party. The attitude of the Belgian hierarchy towards a Fascist régime in Belgium is indicated by the expressive fact that Cardinal van Roey, Archbishop of Malines and Primate of Belgium, officially warned Catholics against participation in the recent World Peace Rally at Brussels, though its discussions and resolutions did not advance beyond moderate Liberalism. Belgium is, evidently, a proximate candidate for the Holy Alliance.

5. *France*.

No exact information can be obtained with regard to the precise relations at present existing between the Church and the French Fascist parties of de la Rocque and Doriot. But French Catholicism, as noted above, is the traditional ally of the older Royalist political reaction. There is no reason to believe that it will act differently with regard to Fascism. Too much importance should not be attached to the condemnation of the proto-Fascist *Action Française* by Pius XI in 1926. Its editors, M. Charles Maurras and M. Léon Daudet, had incurred the anger of Rome by pronouncements of an anti-Catholic nature, particularly upon moral questions. Rome did not condemn the crypto-Fascism, but the anti-Catholic views, of the famous organ of French reaction. A significant pointer at the present time is afforded by the recent condemnation of the *Terre Nouvelle*, the organ of the French Catholics who are co-operating with the Popular Front against Fascism and War. This paper has recently been condemned by ecclesiastical authority and placed on the Index. This would seem to show that French Catholicism is perfectly willing to transfer its traditional alliance with Royalism to the more up-to-date form of reaction represented by Fascism, always provided that, in France, Fascism is willing to regard Paris as " worth a Mass ", and to assume a form favourable to the Church; a " Christian ", and not a Pagan Fascism, as was that of the *Action Française*, which thereby incurred the condemnation of Rome.

It is evident from the facts cited above that the Holy Alliance between the two great reactionary forces of the world to-day, Fascism and Roman Catholicism, is no mere theory or prediction, but is already active and far advanced. As a recent writer aptly remarks : " For the sake of the privileges, educational and financial, which the State grants to the Church, it has chosen to become the recognized ally of a barbaric system, built upon obvious wrong and suffering, thrusting the whole world into an orgy of hate and wars." [1] That this is so, the above facts serve to demonstrate beyond doubt or cavil. It only remains to glance at the purely speculative aspects of this new Holy Alliance before bringing the present enquiry to a final conclusion.

(One can add to the above these equally significant facts : the Papacy and the Japanese Empire have

[1] Edith Moore, *The Political Face of Rome*.

now established mutual diplomatic representation. Evidently the Papacy regards the yellow Empire as a barrier against Red Russia or the possibility of a " Red China ". Cardinal Pacelli, Papal Secretary of State, recently congratulated South America on its return to the Church—via the medium of ruthless repression—involving systematic torture of all advanced movements in Peru, Chile, Brazil, Paraguay, etc.)

CHAPTER V

THE TWO TOTALITARIAN STATES

IN the striking article already quoted, Miss Moore tersely sums up the final aim of the Roman Catholic Church.

" The religious aim of Catholicism is that of saving the souls of all the Heavenly Father's children, or, in blunter terms, the spiritual enslavement of humanity. This constantly demands political action on the part of the Church. For as it cannot possibly rely on the truth of its word for conversion, it is always dependent on the secular power for suppression of those who spread doubt in the minds of its flock." [1]

In other words, the Papacy itself presides over a " Totalitarian " state, a state which claims to dominate, to direct, and to control, in every matter of importance, the thoughts, actions, and political activity of its subjects. It is no accident that the golden age of the Papacy was the theocratic Middle Ages, that its greatest man was Hildebrand, that the proudest day in its long history was the day of Canossa, when it made good a decisive ascendancy over the secular power. Never has the Papacy willingly accepted the subordination imposed upon it by modern conditions. In its

[1] Edith Moore, *ut supra*.

innermost heart it has always cherished the dream
of the renovation of that golden age, when principalities and powers, art and learning, social life
and individual observance alike looked to Rome
as their arche-type and centre. Rome still regards
with complacent approval the prediction of Macaulay, and confidently anticipates that she will survive
"the ruins of St Paul's" and "the broken arch
of London Bridge", and the whole of our modern
civilization, as she has survived so many others.
Semper eadem—"For ever the Same."

Ever optimistic, the Vatican believes, contrary
to all human experience, that it is immune from
human mutability, and that its Golden Age will
come again, the mediæval Age of Faith, when
Rome was the centre of Europe, when politics
existed to promote, art to adorn, and reason to
defend, the Catholic Church, the master of Western
civilization.

The words of consecration addressed to every
Pope as he assumes the tiara are no mummified
survival, but testify to an ambition ever present
in the mind of the Roman theocracy: "Receive
the triple crown, and know that thou art the Father
of kings and princes, the Pastor of the Universe,
and the Vicar on Earth of our Lord Jesus Christ."
The Papacy, however much circumstances may
compel or prudence advise it to veil its real ambitions and to moderate claims that sound ex-
travagant to the modern ear, yet remains in
its innermost essence and conscious ambitions a
theocracy, a totalitarian state. As Harnack truly
said: In the twentieth century, as in the eleventh,
"it is an Empire that this priestly Cæsar rules, it

is just as essential to this church to exercise governmental power as to proclaim the Gospel." [1]

Fascism also is a totalitarian state, which makes similar claims of an all-embracing character, demanding a decisive control of morals, culture, and religion no less than of politics and law. We have already had occasion to refer to the views of its founder, Mussolini, on the " absolute State ". The Fascist state, indeed, is an argus-eyed monster, it realizes in the world of concrete fact the abstract dream of the all-powerful " Leviathan " of absolutist theory. Its effective motto is that expressed in " totalitarian " language as " all within the State, none outside the State, none against the State ". It also demands absolute submission in every sphere of human existence from its subjects. Its ideal for the nation that it rules is that so happily defined by Ludwig Bauer in his classical summary of Fascist Italy :

" Forty million prisoners condemned to perpetual enthusiasm." [2]

Thus the Roman Catholic Church and the Fascist State are both régimes of a totalitarian character. Hence, it is obvious from their essential nature that they are bound eventually to clash. Their relations might ultimately come to resemble those which proverbially subsist between an irresistible force and an immovable obstacle. Incidentally it may be remarked that such friction as has already developed between them is due primarily to the endemic difficulty of harmonizing the

[1] Adolf Harnack, *What is Christianity?*, p. 257.
[2] Ludwig Bauer, *War Again To-morrow*, p. 170.

relations of two claimants to universal domination. It is stark nonsense to assert, as is sometimes done, that the Catholic Church in Germany and elsewhere is defending religious liberty against the Hitler State. As in the days of Bismarck, she is defending her own power.

It may be asserted with complete assurance, and without any aid from necromancy, that the alliance of the Papacy with Fascism must eventually end in a violent rupture just as, and for the same reason as, the alliance of the Papacy with the mediæval Empire ended. *There will, eventually be no room for both*. It is as certain as anything can well be that, once social and intellectual evolution had been arrested, and modern civilization was finally overcome, the world yet again would see re-enacted the drama of Guelf versus Ghibelline, Hildebrand versus Henry IV, Innocent IV versus Frederick Hohenstaufen, the violent clash of the "Two Swords", of the State versus the Church.

"When modern civilization was finally overcome": There we have the preliminary condition for the breach between Fascism and Rome. As long as it stands, the allies need each other too badly to afford a quarrel. From the standpoint of the Papacy, even a Totalitarian State is better than a "godless" one, the necessary conclusion of modern evolution. From the standpoint of Fascism even Rome is better than Reason. In the last desperate stand of the forces of political and cultural darkness, Beelzebub and Apollyon must needs stand side by side. Rome is now too weak to stand alone; she cannot to-day dispense with the aid of Fascism.

It still remains true, however, that " the needs of the Church override every other law ". In the twentieth century the Church needs Fascism, as in the ninth it needed Charlemagne. But once the Lombards were out of the way, it did not need his successors. Were the march of modern civilization once arrested, it would not need the successors of the Fascist dictators of to-day. The Papacy is the most totalitarian of all totalitarian States, since it embraces heaven equally with earth and its writ runs even on the farther side of death. It can never swear *eternal* friendship with a rival totalitarian State. With such a régime only a marriage of convenience is possible, and a marriage, at that, dictated by urgent reasons !

It is evident that Rome alone of contemporary religious bodies possesses sufficient strength to offer herself as an ally to the contemporary reaction. Protestantism has always been too dependent on Capitalism to take up an independent attitude towards it. It was no accident that the classical economists of the capitalist heyday confidently declared that " Jesus Christ is Free Trade ", or that Calvin was the first theologian to defend usury, in defiance of the mediæval ban which reflected the stagnant economics of the feudal system. Protestantism, in fact, never had any religious vitality apart from modern economics and their consequent ethics. It is again no accident that it was only at the Reformation that punctuality, *the* essential capitalist virtue, was declared to be a *religious* virtue. The proletarian who is late at the factory gate cannot be in time at the door of heaven ! To-day, in so far as Protestantism still remains alive, it shows a disposition to repeat humbly the *obiter dicta* of the Vatican.[1] As for the Russian Orthodox church, "Where are the snows of yesterday?"; melted in the fire of revolution! Victor Hugo long ago foretold that, when the ice did eventually break on the Neva, much else would break besides. As for the churches of the Reformation, the demagogue Hitler would appear to have finished the church which the demagogue Luther began; and the grim Calvin is now repudiated by everyone, and by no one more than by the free churches, which were originally Calvinist in doctrine. Only Rome is left as the standard bearer of the religious reaction standing defiantly against the modern world, able to offer her alliance to the similarly conditioned political reaction generically styled "Fascism".

I have elsewhere summarized the relations hitherto existent between the Church of Rome and modern capitalist civilization.

"Broadly, it can be said that the relations of the bourgeois order to the Roman Catholic Church have passed through two main stages. In the first stage, that of the rise of the bourgeoisie at the conclusion of the Middle Ages, the church, as the close ally of Feudalism, fought against the new social order with every means in its power. Even its persecutions had a social character. It burned Bruno and silenced Galileo on account of astronomical discoveries which forwarded navigation, the supreme instrument of bourgeois world-expansion in the epoch of

[1] See Note HH, p. 254.

the Voyages of Discovery. It endeavoured, also, to prohibit the use of gunpowder, the weapon with which the early bourgeois revolutionaries broke down the supremacy of the feudal horse-men, and battered down the hitherto impregnable walls of the mediæval castles.

"Eventually, however, the Capitalist order was too strong for it, and it was forced, re-luctantly enough, to compromise. It recognized the new mathematics, and, therewith, the helio-centric theories which it had formerly con-demned. More important, it was forced to compound with capitalist finance, with the mediæval 'sin of usury' without which no bourgeois order is even conceivable. Even the Holy Days of the Saints (which, by reason of their excessive numbers, were a hindrance to the new order of production) became the Holy-days (Holidays) of the Banks.

"These concessions, however, were not made except as the sole alternative to a struggle which the *savoir faire* of the Catholic Church demon-strated at that time to be hopeless. The Roman religion is an agricultural religion, whose Deity is incarnate in the twin pillars of Latin agri-culture, bread and wine. Land and Church, alike, change too slowly to welcome that dogma of 'progress' which was the credo of the new industrial order. Moreover, the Roman Catholic Church, 'the last creative masterpiece of An-tiquity', as a modern theologian has aptly styled it, had inherited too much from the Roman Empire to be content with the subordinate position, which was all that the bourgeoisie

assigned to it. (It was not for nothing that
Thomas Hobbes, the most penetrating of English
political philosophers, wrote in *Leviathan* (1651)
that ' the Papacy is the ghost of the Roman
Empire sitting crowned on the grave thereof.')

" Now, with the evident decay of the Capitalist
order, Rome sees its opportunity of a new
epoch of power, wherein the era of Hildebrand
and of Canossa will return. The decline of the
once arrogantly confident bourgeois order is
now exemplified by its recourse in ever-increasing
measure to the open atavism that is represented
in every sphere by Fascism, the open negation
of ' progress ' both in fact and in world philosophy. To Rome, Communism is a Utopian
Myth. Georges Sorel, in *Reflections on Violence*,
said truly enough that the sacerdotal caste is
of all social classes the most alien to the men-
tality of the producers. Hence, Rome prepares
either to supersede the bourgeois order altogether,
or at least to force upon it her own conditions
of alliance against the forces of the social revolution which threaten both.

" The recent Papal Encyclical, May 15, 1931,
attacking both Capitalism and Communism, can
only be understood in this sense. For this
purpose, she possesses assets that are exceedingly
formidable. In an age of mass organization, her
own splendid organization must count. In a
cosmopolitan age her own unrivalled experience
must tell. To know one's own mind in a shaken
world is itself no small asset. Her vast experience
has taught her all that there is to know about the
constant aspect of human nature, the variable or

evolutionary aspect she does not know nearly as well." [1]

Such is the alliance, and such the allies who consummate their union in the twentieth century; who, driven on by the inner logic of their world rôle, aim consciously at the destruction of the immediate enemy, socialism, and deliberately proceed to destroy the whole rationalist, secular, and scientific civilization which to-day culminates in the social and scientific evolution of the twentieth century. The Catholic-Fascist Alliance, the Holy Alliance of the two black internationals, represents the last stand of the Middle Ages. Its definitive triumph would not, and could not, stop short of a complete return to the mediæval age which is its spiritual home, and of the complete liquidation of modern civilization. The victory of Fascism over social progress would be paralleled by the triumph of Rome over Reason.

"That way madness lies". Should the evil thing come to pass, and the most monstrous retrogression in history be, after all, accomplished, then, along with the Middle Ages, will return its conflict of theocracy versus the secular state, the war of the "two swords", in which Rome, as by far the more homogeneous and experienced combatant, could easily prevail, as she prevailed in former days over the Holy Roman Empire, which the Papacy preceded, created, and survived.

But first, before the era of the mediæval Popes returns, the Middle Ages must emerge from their

---

[1] *Cf.* F. A. Ridley, " The New Adelphi, January, 1933, pp. 238-40—*Marx, Aristotle and the Black International.*

tomb and clamber back to their former seats of power. And for that to occur, some vital centuries must be expunged altogether from the human register. Mankind and its civilization must, yet again, tread the road that leads to Canossa.

Note HH : Rome and the non-Catholic Churches

In so far as the non-Catholic Churches still take up a logical—*i.e.* reactionary—position, they walk humbly in the wake of Rome. Lutheran synods echo the Papal diatribes against " the menace of Communism ", the Archbishop of Canterbury denounces the doings of " godless Russia " in accents that are but a pale reflection of the robust anathemas of Pius XI. Even the staunchly Protestant " Society for the Promotion of Christian Knowledge " prefaces its translation of Mgr. d'Herbigny's comprehensive and full-blooded denunciation of Communism with the approving introductory remark :

" The S.P.C.K. welcomes the opportunity of presenting to the English-speaking public this fully-documented description by Mgr. d'Herbigny of the world-wide attack upon religion and the notable part played by the Roman Catholic Church in the defence of the Christian Faith " [1]

A generation ago, such a tribute to Rome from a Protestant propagandist organization like the S.P.C.K. would have been incredible. The occurrence of such phenomena shows how decisively the religious reaction now centres in Rome.

---

[1] *Cf. Militant Atheism—The Worldwide Propaganda of Communism*, by the Right Rev. Mgr. Michel d'Herbigny, Bishop of Ilium and President of the Pontifical Commission on Russia.

Chapter VI

MUST EUROPEAN CIVILIZATION GO TO CANOSSA?

WILL Western Civilization go to Canossa? It certainly will if the Holy Alliance gets its way. It is not intrinsically impossible that Western civilization may relapse into Balkanization, or even into the downright barbarism of a new Dark Age, a fate which the upholders of certain current philosophies of history already confidently predict for modern Europe, as once for its classical predecessor. Certainly the idea of progress carries with it the complementary idea of retrogression as its necessary obverse and counterpart.[1]

It would be difficult in our tortured and disillusioned generation to find an echo of the complacent optimism of the smug Victorians, for while the tendency of evolution is undoubtedly towards human improvement, and, we may suppose, human perfection, it is unfortunately not so certain as the generation of Herbert Spencer supposed that " mankind must become perfect ". Current history is full of counter-tendencies, and a crossroad, rather than a direct highway, represents its apposite symbol.[2]

Consequently the road to the Middle Ages is still open, the road backwards. It is, indeed, the

[1] *Cf.* J. B. Bury, *The Idea of Progress.*
[2] *Cf.* F. A. Ridley, *At the Cross Roads of History.*

unique characteristic of our generation that, like the Roman God of Time, Janus, it presents two faces to the world, one to the age of science and plenty that lies before ; the other to the age of scarcity and superstition that lies behind. To transpose the algebra of historical philosophy into the arithmetic of current political activity, the former is represented by such forward-looking social experiments as those at present being conducted in such countries as Russia, Mexico and Spain, the latter is embodied in the contemporary reaction and, very particularly, in those spiritual and political forces which, not content with seeking to stabilize the institutions of the present, seek to return to the outmoded customs of the past.

Of these reactionary forces in contemporary life the present Holy Alliance between Fascism and the Papacy is by far the strongest, the most aggressive, and the most logical in its comprehensive atavism. Not content with striking down its contemporary enemies, the current forces of human progress, it traces them to their roots far back in history, and it seeks out those roots in order to destroy them.

The feature which pre-eminently characterizes the Holy Alliance, and distinguishes it from the other, merely empirical, reactionary forces of to-day, is that it is a conspiracy to destroy not merely the shoots, but the roots of modern life ; once again, it is modern civilization itself which is its destined victim. The whole stupendous period of modern culture that separates the era of Caxton and Columbus from our own, that mighty age of unprecedented intellectual expansion which, with whatever incidental crimes and follies, has unlocked the temple of knowledge to the human race and has placed an age of Justice and Plenty within its reach, is to be expunged entirely, is to become a *tabula rasa* in the history of humanity, if the alliance of Fascism and Catholicism achieves its purpose. Logically, and the allies are, both, essentially logical, this can only mean the return to the Middle Ages, to the age of Faith and Ignorance before modern civilization. This is the road that leads straight to Canossa.

Will modern civilization take that road? That depends both upon the degree of awareness which its component parts possess, and upon the degree of unity which they can in consequence achieve in face of the common peril. One thing at least is certain, they all have everything at stake. Man stands to-day on the threshold of the age of plenty, of a new chapter in human history. In order that he may enter upon his inheritance, hitherto only glimpsed from afar, the dead hand of the past, and its obstructing fetters, must be finally removed. Only thus can he enter into the Promised Land; only thus can humanity rise from the level of the irrational and the mythological to that of the rational and the real; only thus can mankind emerge from the dark tunnel of chaos and confusion in which it now wanders, into the tranquil light and harmonious splendour of the coming dawn.

EPILOGUE—"SEMPER EADEM"

> " Seize the first Apostle's sword,
>   Peter's glowing sword, and smite !
>   Scatter far the savage horde ;
>   Break their wild impetuous might.
>   Let them feel the yoke of yore,
>   Let them bear it evermore ! "

(Exhortation of Italian Prelate to Pope Gregory VII, *the Founder of the Mediaeval Papacy*.)

Semper eadem, "For ever the Same"; this now as in the past, remains the unchanging motto of the Papacy. It is in the spirit of these haughty words that she faces the crisis of the twentieth century, as she has faced the successive crises of bygone days. She seeks in the deep and well-stored recesses of her profound memories for the precedents and examples which have served her so well in the past, and which she hopes to imitate in relation to the crisis which at present faces her.

Nor does she fail to find them in the course of a history so full of storm and stress as hers has been throughout the nineteen centuries of constant battle which separates the generation of St Peter from that of Pius XI.

It would be altogether misleading to suppose that there is anything new in the eyes of the Papacy either in the crisis which at present confronts it, or in the expedient of seeking and finding allies in the secular world, whose interests and hatreds coincide with its own. Pius XI, who calls the Fascists to his aid in the twentieth century, only repeats the example of Gregory VII nine centuries ago, who similarly called on the Normans. If the Fascists are entirely reactionary, whereas the Normans were, on the whole, a progressive force in the world of their day, this signifies only the increasing atavism of the Papacy, as modern civilization progresses farther and farther beyond the standards of the Middle Ages.

The policy pursued by Rome in the face of the crisis of our century does not differ in any essential respect from the policy she pursued when faced with the earlier crises which she has already surmounted in the centuries that have fled, and whose vivid imprint is still stamped upon her tenacious memory. *Semper eadem*; she seeks in the past for her technique and her models when confronted by the circumstances of the present age of social and of intellectual revolution.

She does not seek in vain ! The past rises up so vividly from the deeps of the unconscious that the present becomes transfigured and revivified in the light of what has gone before. She lives again in the bygone centuries, the scenes of the past recur, old shades start up, old champions rise from their tombs and repeat in her service, and at her behest, deeds at which the world has long shuddered, and which it fondly thought it had left behind for good and all. Once again the Papacy calls in Charlemagne, the founder of the Holy Roman Empire, reincarnated as Mussolini, the Founder of the New Rome, which will save the old from destruction ; once again a new Simon de Montfort, in the person of General Franco, mercilessly harries the enemies of the

Church with fire and sword, as his mediæval predecessor exterminated the Albigenses ; once again the bells of Rome are rung, and bonfires burn to celebrate the new St Bartholomew's Eve, the massacre of the victims of Vienna, of Addis Ababa, of Badajoz, Malaga and Madrid, by the chosen champions and emissaries of the church, with her blessing and consent ; once again the Pope raises the battle-cry, *Deus vult*——" It is the Will of Heaven "—as Hitler, the successor and antitype of Godfrey de Bouillon, gathers the embattled hosts of " Christian civilization " for the final crusade against " the enemies of Christ and of Christendom ", the Russian " Anti-Christ " to the East.

The silver trumpets of the Vatican are blowing with no uncertain sound ; the past rises up to confront the present, and the battle is already joined in Spain. It is a war without quarter or compromise, a war of light against darkness, a war of modern civilization against mediæval barbarism, a war of science versus superstition, above all, it is a war of the Future against the Past, for upon its ultimate issue depends the fate of Humanity and of human civilization.

THE END

INDEX

60335